W9-BYL-115

Charting Your Course

Lessons Learned During the Journey Toward Performance Excellence

Also Available from ASQ Quality Press

Insights to Performance Excellence in Education 2003: An Inside Look at the 2003 Baldrige Award Criteria for Education
Mark L. Blazey, Karen S. Davison, and John P. Evans

Improving Student Learning: Applying Deming's Quality Principles in Classrooms, Second Edition
Lee Jenkins

Successful Applications of Quality Systems in K–12 Schools
ASQ Education Division

Futuring Tools for Strategic Quality Planning in Education
William F. Alexander and Richard W. Serfass

Living on the Edge of Chaos: Leading Schools into the Global Age
Karolyn J. Snyder, Michel Acker-Hocevar, and Kristen M. Snyder

Orchestrating Learning with Quality
David P. Langford and Barbara Cleary

Tools and Techniques to Inspire Classroom Learning
Barbara A. Cleary, Ph.D. and Sally J. Duncan

Thinking Tools for Kids: An Activity Book for Classroom Learning
Barbara A. Cleary, Ph.D. and Sally J. Duncan

School Self-Assessment Guide for Performance Excellence
ASQ Koalaty Kid

From Baldrige to the Bottom Line: A Road Map for Organizational Change and Improvement
David W. Hutton

Orchestrating Learning with Quality
Langford, David P. and Cleary, Barbara A., Ph.D.

Charting Your Course

Lessons Learned During the Journey Toward Performance Excellence

John G. Conyers and Robert Ewy

ASQ Quality Press
Milwaukee, Wisconsin

Charting Your Course Lessons Learned During the Journey Toward Performance Excellence
John G. Conyers and Robert Ewy

Library of Congress Cataloging-in-Publication Data

Conyers, John G., 1945-
Charting your course : lessons learned during the journey toward
performance excellence / John G. Conyers and Robert Ewy.
p. cm.
Includes bibliographical references and index.
ISBN 0-87389-607-6 (hardcover : alk. paper)
1. School management and organization. 2. School improvement
programs. 3. Organizational effectiveness. I. Ewy, Robert, 1940- II.
Title.
LB2805.C639 2003
371.2--dc22
2003021343

10 9 8 7 6 5 4 3 2

ISBN 0-87389-607-6

Acquisitions Editor: Annemieke Hytinen
Project Editor: Paul O'Mara
Production Administrator: Randy Benson
Special Marketing Representative: David Luth

ASQ Mission: The American Society for Quality advances individual and organizational
performance excellence worldwide by providing opportunities for learning, quality
improvement, and knowledge exchange.

Printed in the United States of America

Printed on acid-free paper

Quality Press
600 N. Plankinton Avenue
Milwaukee, Wisconsin 53203
Call toll free 800-248-1946
Fax 414-272-1734
www.asq.org
http://qualitypress.asq.org
http://standardsgroup.asq.org
E-mail: authors@asq.org

Table of Contents

Foreword

A little note about the organization of this book.

We have chosen to entitle this book *Charting Your Course* because the Malcolm Baldrige criteria are nonprescriptive. The criteria do not tell you what to do—you have the leeway to chart your own course. What Baldrige does is give you a systematic framework for organizational excellence. How you bring it about is dependent on your leadership.

Throughout this book you will see a number of nautical and marine references. Why? Because it is in mariner lore, knowledge, and understanding that we have found many analogies to organizational excellence. In our days of classroom teaching, we often used colorful examples to make our lessons more vivid, memorable, and understandable. We have included these nautical interpretations for the same reasons.

Picture yourself on a boat in a lovely tropical harbor, ready to anchor and stay for a while. The integral rule for anchoring is that the chain or the anchor rode or line should be at a 7:1 ratio. Only then can you relax and feel firm in the knowledge that you are anchored/rooted at the end of your journey. You will find that the same anchor strength can be found in the seven categories of the Malcolm Baldrige criteria:

1. Leadership
2. Strategic Planning
3. Student, Stakeholder, and Market Focus
4. Measurement, Analysis, Knowledge Management

5. Faculty and Staff Focus
6. Process Management
7. Organizational Performance Results

(A list of our nautical reference sources is shown on page 153.)

Preface: Casting Off

For Community Consolidated School District 15, charting our course began one afternoon a few years ago when a community member brought to my attention a Motorola brochure that had been disseminated to all the company's employees worldwide. Thumbing through it, I was very disturbed! The document implied that America's role as a leader in the global marketplace was at risk unless the American K-12 education system was improved, and quickly!

Motorola's then chairman and chief executive officer, Robert Galvin, made the time to talk to me. I came right to the point: "Are you concerned about the schools' product? I need to know, because I found this brochure quite alarming." Mr. Galvin's reply was incisive. For Motorola to continue to compete successfully on a global scale, he said, the students who would become its future employees must be trained to compete in world-class global competition. As our conversation continued, I was struck by Mr. Galvin's intense fervor for Motorola's "Six Sigma" quality system. Six Sigma, he explained, originally created as a continuous quality improvement technique, had evolved into an overall high performance system that drives the company's business strategy. On the way back to my office, I affirmed to myself that we as a district needed that same fervor—that same level of commitment to quality for our primary and extended customers. *The passion that drives us as educators—disciplined with criteria for pursuing excellence—is what we owe our children, our communities, our economy, our future.*

The Helm is the function of steering the ship, thereby controlling her direction. Ashore, a helmsman is a person who is at the helm, that is, in a position of control.

Back in the office, I sat down with Bob Ewy, District 15's director of planning. "We have to address the issue of systematic quality improvement across the district," I remember telling him. Bob quickly and enthusiastically agreed, and together we started to strategize about what that meant and how we could implement it. It was then that I asked him to assume the position of "Helmsman of Quality," working under my direction and in concert with me with authority to keep us on our course to performance excellence.

We felt we were a good school district, and we worked hard to maintain the support and trust of our community while pursuing performance excellence. We could point to thousands of examples of excellence throughout the district—what we later came to recognize as "random acts of excellence"—but the overall results were not especially remarkable. An unshakable commitment to districtwide quality that would continue to improve over time was the bottom line that was missing in our board of education goals and our accountability to the community.

As a board member on several local chambers of commerce, I had access to the business community and began discussing this issue with selected individuals. What I eventually realized was that schools (not just ours, but all public schools) were stigmatized because of the perception that we used "soft criteria" and had less accountability to our customers than effective business organizations do. It was a troubling discovery, and I instructed our staff to begin looking for higher standards of accountability that could be applied to our district's performance at all levels. We made the choice to stop accepting excuses, to hold ourselves to a higher level of accountability, and to be more open and honest with our community about our planned journey to become a first-rate, world-class organization.

After extensive research, we decided to "chart our course" using the Malcolm Baldrige criteria to help in the development of a results-driven, systemic approach to organizational improvement. Only the Baldrige framework truly met the world-class standards that we were looking for. Little did we know how difficult—yet how absolutely fascinating—this journey would be.

We are now well along our charted course toward continuous improvement. Although it is a journey that never ends, we can proudly point to some important achievements:

- We are now a mission-driven district, from the overall district mission set by the board of education to those written by students in individual classrooms in our 19 schools.
- The prevailing style of management has been changed from top-down directive to shared decision-making and consensus building.
- Continuous improvement has become a core value across the district.
- We pride ourselves on management by fact, meaning we measure everything important so we can track our progress along the way. We jokingly say that, "If it moves, measure it!" to make the point about the importance of the core value of management by fact.

In the pages that follow, we share with you our journey, the charting of our course. When we began, few other school districts had attempted this. We could find no guidebook, few examples, and certainly no step-by-step directions. We had to work our own way through the process ... but we believe our experience can offer you some valuable, time- and trouble-saving guidance. We share some of our results, and humbly and candidly tell you of the things that went wrong in the hope you can learn from our mistakes and use that knowledge to avoid disappointment and duress during your organization's quality journey. We do not think for a moment that District 15 has all the answers to achieving high performance, but we have had state and national Baldrige examiners verify that we have figured out many answers that work. Your task in reading this book is to decide if you think our answers might work for you.

BY AND LARGE: THE SAILORS' DESCRIPTION OF A PASSAGE WHICH INCLUDED BAD DAYS OF HEADWINDS WHEN THE SHIP WOULD HAVE TO BE SAILED BY THE WIND, AND GOOD DAYS WHEN THE LARGE SAILS COULD BE USED TO GIVE GREATER SPEED AND COMFORT TO THE VESSEL.
–*SALTY DOG TALK, P. 14*

As the president of the District 15 Board of Education, Louis A. Sands, says, "We are firm believers that the application of the Baldrige criteria has changed our school district tremendously, and our community would endorse that conviction."

We would not presume to say to you that our course would be your journey. Your journey to excellence must be your own.

As Olivia Isil says in her delightful book, *When a Loose Cannon Flogs a Dead Horse There's the Devil to Pay*, "Now, with bearing set, and navigational charts in hand, embark on a short sail or a long voyage through the sea of words that awaits. Conditions may sometimes be foggy, but, by and large, smooth sailing is in the offing."

—John G. Conyers

Authors' Addendum: As this book went to press, District 15 was in the process of a site visit from Baldrige examiners in October 2003—one more milestone in the demanding Baldrige process.

Acknowledgements

This book is dedicated to the more than 2,000 wonderful men and women who come to work every day committed to continuous improvement for the 13,000 students of Community Consolidated School District 15.

A special note of thanks to seven exceptional members of the District 15 Board of Education who believed that world-class standards could actually be attained through the use of Malcolm Baldrige criteria to achieve performance excellence: Mr. Lou Sands, president; Dr. Laura Crane, vice president; and Mrs. Paula Mikula, Mrs. Linda Silverman, Mr. Edward Yung, Mrs. Nancy Carlson, and Mr. Scott Boucher.

A special note to our tenacious chief editor, Carol Nelson, who gave us her time unselfishly to professionally critique and superbly edit our work. Her efforts helped give this book the honesty and continuity in the story of our quality journey.

We are particularly indebted to our wonderful wives, Jean and Christine, who provided deep and thoughtful support of our work with their critiques, ideas, and above all, encouragement . . . and to our great executive assistants, Pat Campbell, Debbie Ross, and Debbie Hughes . . . and thanks to our critical friends who provided support, encouragement, and feedback for the journey: Motorola Corporation, Northrop Grumman, Carol Ann Rush, Lincoln Foundation for Business Excellence, and Margaret Byrnes . . . and to my mother, Bernice Conyers, who was laid to rest Sept. 11, 2003, at age 86. She taught me the joy of reading, writing, and speaking with the parental expectation that all her boys were to strive for excellence in everything they do.

John G. Conyers
Robert Ewy

1

Pursuing First-Rate Organizational Excellence: Is It Worth the Effort?

What determines how great an organization will become is a leadership system with clear and measurable organizational values, directions, and expectations. It is not by chance that Category 1 of the Baldrige criteria is focused on leadership. And it is not by chance that the focus is on how leaders set, communicate, and deploy, as the Baldrige criteria specifies, "organizational values, short- and longer-term directions, and performance expectations."

This is where senior leaders step up and declare exactly how great the organization is going to become and how they are going to lead it there. This is where senior leaders get the mission and vision thing right . . . or not.

We HAVE MET THE ENEMY AND THEY ARE OURS.
—*Oliver H. Perry, War of 1812*

We believe the basic challenge to senior leaders in educational organizations is that there are no excuses for not moving ahead. If we still had any excuses for not leading our district and schools toward a high-performing future, international consultant Peter Block took them away when he said:

> *We need to stop asking "how?" We now have all the knowledge, the skills, the methods, the tools, the capacity, and the freedom to do whatever is required to serve all students well. All that is needed is the will and courage to choose and to move on.*[1]

The challenge of teaching all students and closing the gap in student achievement will not go away, even if No

Child Left Behind (NCLB) legislation does. We can choose to ignore this glaring problem and point our fingers of blame at others, or we can choose to do something about it. One important thing Block didn't mention is that the leaders/managers must be the first to demonstrate the will and courage to move the district forward. Senior leaders who have this kind of will and courage are not common, but extraordinary. The mere fact that you are reading this book indicates you are one of those rare leaders who agree we have run out of excuses and need to move forward ... that you have the will and courage to move ahead quickly so that no student need suffer any longer in a poor or mediocre learning environment.

WHAT SCHOOLS HAVE NOT DONE SO FAR IS PRODUCE STUDENTS WHOSE ACHIEVEMENT ISN'T PREDICTED BY SOCIO-ECONOMIC STATUS.
–*JAMES TRAUB*[2]

The problem of discernible gaps in student achievement has gone on long enough—and it is unacceptable. The President of the United States has said it ... the Secretary of Education has said it ... superintendents and boards of education say it, and any educator with a conscience will say it. In our district, we have a specific student performance target to address this issue:

> *There is no significant difference between student groups in meeting or exceeding all Illinois learning standards for students who have been in the district for more than one year.*

We are closing in on this target, and this book will help you understand how we are doing it. One thing we are clear about is that it's a cynical excuse to blame our primary customers—our students—for our failures. We have to move our good intentions to action, beyond the excuses about why we can't separate socioeconomic status and achievement. It is the ethical thing to do.

DAMN THE TORPEDOES! FULL SPEED AHEAD!
–*DAVID FARRAGUT, CIVIL WAR*

The next few pages will offer our advice on how to move ahead—and moving ahead, we think, is the only truly moral or ethical decision to make.

The Will *(as in, "They set to work with a will and in a determined and energetic way."—Webster)*

In most of the world, dissatisfied customers simply go elsewhere to get goods and services that meet or hopefully exceed their requirements. In public education, that is not possible, except in rare occasions (charter schools, voucher programs, and so on). It therefore becomes the moral responsibility of senior leaders to advocate for the "customer"—in effect, to become the voice of the customer.

Generally speaking, we know what our customers want. There's nothing subtle in their expectations. They want an excellent education for their sons or daughters, nothing less. Mediocrity is not acceptable. How we meet our customers' requirements can be a complex problem, but determining their requirements is not hard.

Providing an excellent education requires an excellent organization, because students clearly can't receive an excellent education in a mediocre organization. Ensuring organizational excellence is the responsibility and moral obligation of senior leaders. Senior leaders are the only people in the organization with a whole system perspective, positional power, and the resource control needed to determine both strategy and action.

Senior leaders in education are entrusted with the destiny of their organization, which in turn determines the destiny of the organization's students. That is why senior leaders in education have more than just a job—they have the responsibility of creating life-long destinies for students. We don't believe for a moment what Coleman and others said about the school not making a difference.[3] We are convinced that ineffective school systems create an academic legacy of inadequate learning.

THE DIRECTION IN WHICH EDUCATION STARTS A MAN WILL DETERMINE HIS FUTURE LIFE.
—*PLATO*

It is very difficult to have effective schools and teachers in an ineffective district system, and, if you find them, they are isolated examples. As we show in Chapter 9, students whose teachers create ineffective classroom systems (especially two or three years in a row) do not recover from the academic deficit that causes. That is why a leader's job is to optimize systems, as W. Edwards Deming describes, although that's not the usual job description for school administrators and teacher leaders.

There is, though, a very compelling opposing point of view that you need to understand well, because you have to be ready for it when it inevitably comes up. Not all constituents (for example, parents, students, community members) agree that greatness/excellence is necessary or even an admirable goal. Some are not willing to support what it takes to get there, and they won't be reserved about expressing their views. "We are good enough" is an often-heard statement. A variation is, "We have done just fine in the past. Why do we need to change now?"

It's a problem that senior leaders of educational organizations who declare they are committed to greatness or excellence are confronted with daily, related to almost every decision they make. There's one simple question that has profound implications for the leader and the organization: "Do you want your organization to be good or great?" A less gentle way of asking the question is, "Do you want your organization to be mediocre or excellent?" The answer to the question, one would assume, would always be greatness or excellence. In truth, it seldom is.

Without powerful data-based answers to these questions, you will not able to move forward. You will, in fact, be getting too far in front of your constituents for your own professional health. Senior leaders put themselves at considerable risk by getting too far in front of their constituents. Those who do update their resumes frequently.

Students who have been getting along doing a minimal amount of work for a reasonably good grade are not particularly pleased by a new commitment to excellence because it means a very different set of standards are applied to what is taught and the evidence used to judge student performance. Unions frequently have commitments to security and the status quo, not performance excellence. There is much for a senior leader to confront when moving an organization to the next level. It is so much easier to manage the organization as it is, put in a few improvements here and there (the proverbial "random acts of improvement"), and go home at night with everyone feeling quite good.

To make the statement that average performance is not good enough and to confront the necessity of changing systems (personnel, information, assessment, decision-making, and curriculum) in order to move to greatness is a decision many senior leaders, in private as well as public organizations, just don't want to make.

YOU MAY FIRE WHEN READY, GRIDLEY.

—GEORGE DEWEY, SPANISH-AMERICAN WAR

The Courage *(as in "having the courage of one's convictions, to be brave enough to do what one feels to be right."—Webster)*

It takes courage to be willing to confront fundamental problems faced by senior leaders in education. One problem is that there are few incentives available to senior leaders to improve student performance, except under extreme circumstances that trigger state or federal sanctions like those written into the NCLB legislation.

Motivation strategies that the corporate world relies on just do not exist in educational organizations. For example, *Fortune* magazine each year lists the 100 best companies to work for and describes what makes them so great. Besides the obvious incentives of bonuses and stock options, some companies offer domestic partner benefits, free yoga classes, and massages. Zero or no-layoff policies, paid sabbaticals, linking health insurance premiums to compensation (the less you earn, the less you pay), state-of-the-art workout gyms, cafeterias, tuition reimbursement with no cap, and mortgage assistance are just some of the incentives used to enhance motivation and increase personal performance.

When, as in a monopoly, there is no direct relationship between meeting or exceeding customer needs and the organization's survival, a very powerful "status quo" attitude can pervade the entire organization. The "good enoughers" are out there in full force and you have limited incentives at your disposal to overcome them or bring about a shift in attitude.

Rarely are administrators' and teachers' careers and future employment dependent upon the performance of students in their school or district. To the contrary: Pay and promotion for both teachers and administrators are usually independent of how the teacher or school does at increasing student performance. How many teachers or administrators do you know who have been reprimanded or lost their jobs because they didn't increase student performance? The majority of teachers and schools do well enough that they don't show up on the radar screen that identifies mediocre or poor performers. They can be just "good enough" for an entire career. Unfortunately, "good enough" performance will not get your organization to great.

We have found ourselves in constant comparisons between schools and businesses. Schools are a business, a big business … and if we in education chart our course using the highest evaluative criteria available (the Baldrige criteria), we can maintain our course for kids. We don't have to wait for answers from others.

It takes courage to ask an external group of examiners into your district to do a careful and complete audit of your major systems. It takes courage to share that audit with staff and community members, no matter what the result. It takes courage to begin disaggregating test score data by teacher and act on the results. Here are a few questions to test your own levels of will and courage:

- Are you ready to confront the possibility that the systems currently in place in the organization, perhaps some that you designed, are creating mediocre results or not achieving the organization's true potential?
- Are you ready to address the issue that to achieve the kind of organizational excellence you aspire to, you may not have the right people in leadership positions, even if those people have become professional friends?
- Do you truly understand that creating organizational excellence is not a popularity contest but is being an advocate for the least politically powerful subgroups of students?
- Do you have the will to impose greater responsibility on staff and greater accountability on the organization, even though you know you may meet with considerable resistance?

We can't give you will or courage ... but we recognize that you would not be a senior leader if you were not prepared to courageously command the helm. However, willing and courageous leaders who are successful are armed with more than just their convictions. Even people with courage need knowledge, skill, tools, and expertise to exercise effective leadership in setting values, directions, and expectations and to integrate them into a culture that has a passion for excellence.

This book has been written as an extended case study that describes our stumbles, struggles, and successes in our journey and suggests some strategies and tactics that can help you continue your focus on organizational excellence. We know you have the will and courage to take the challenge, so read on!

ENDNOTES

1. Block, Peter. 1998. Consortium for Educational Change Summer Institute Presentation.
2. Traub, James. 2000. "What No School Can Do," *The New York Times Magazine* (16 January).
3. Coleman, James S. 1966. *Equality of educational opportunity.* Washington, D.C., National Center for Educational Statistics.

2

The America's Cup Challenge: Why the Baldrige Criteria?

Why the Baldrige criteria? Because nothing can move an organization forward more quickly than applying the Baldrige criteria.

That's a bold statement, but most people who have studied organization improvement frameworks would tend to agree. Those of us in Community Consolidated School District 15 who have been driving the continuous quality improvement process for the past several years are convinced that it is true.

When we began our quest for districtwide quality improvement, we looked hard for a set of first-rate criteria that could serve as a framework for our efforts.

We knew a *systemwide* approach to continuous improvement was needed. School districts often regard themselves as a sum of their separate parts—their schools. When you're seeking an organizationwide improvement in quality, you can't take that view. A school-by-school approach that invokes individual random acts of excellence clearly isn't the key to attaining systemic improvement. We knew that we would have to change our thinking so that we consistently looked at the district as a single system—a complex one, but a single system nonetheless.

Typically, school districts don't use a *systems perspective* to develop solutions. Unfortunately, thinking about a systems perspective to organizational improvement when you're up to your neck in alligators in the swamp of everyday activities is not easy. Still, we realized that the very complexity of our organization demanded a framework that would help us think

THE AMERICA'S CUP: IN 1851 THE AMERICAN SCHOONER AMERICA WON THE 100 GUINEA CUP FOR A RACE AROUND THE ISLE OF WIGHT. THE CUP WAS LATER PRESENTED TO THE NEW YORK YACHT CLUB AS A PRIZE TO BE CONTENDED FOR BY THE HOLDERS AND ANY FOREIGN YACHT CLUB. SEVENTEEN YEARS LATER, JAMES ASHBURY, VICE COMMODORE OF THE ROYAL HARWICH YACHT CLUB CHALLENGED, AND SO STARTED WHAT HAS BECOME THE MOST PRESTIGIOUS AND COMPETITIVE SPORTING EVENT EVER.

–THE SAILOR'S HANDBOOK P. 162

FIRST-RATE: THE MIGHTY WARSHIPS OF THE BRITISH ROYAL NAVY WERE ONCE RATED ON THEIR SIZE, ORDINANCE, AND HOPEFULLY, EFFECTIVENESS. THE NAVAL RATING SYSTEM WAS ASSIMILATED INTO EVERYDAY USAGE TO DESCRIBE DEGREES OF EXCELLENCE.

–WHEN A LOOSE CANNON FLOGS A DEAD HORSE THERE'S THE DEVIL TO PAY, P. 37

about the district in its entirety, assess our strengths and weaknesses, and enable us to focus our time and attention on the specific things that needed improvement.

Only the Baldrige criteria truly met our needs. Here's why:

- The Baldrige framework is universally applicable, an approach that can be applied to any business or organization.
- It is internationally known and respected as the hallmark of quality.
- It is a rigorous but attainable set of core values and criteria for performance excellence.
- It is a powerful self-assessment tool.
- It helps organizations build capacity to accelerate and sustain continuous improvement.

Organizational guru Stephen Covey notes that all organizations are perfectly aligned to get the results they get. He alleges that misalignment is one of the major problems in organizations.

That's true of our organization and yours, too. Think about the good results you're satisfied with, even proud of. You have aligned your organization to get those good results. Now, think about the results that don't make you so happy. Isn't it probable that your organization is also aligned to get those results in the same way you are aligned to get the good results?

We chose the Baldrige criteria as our realignment framework. If you're serious about improving performance across your entire organization, it would be a wise choice for you, too.

Why Baldrige Works

IN THE BALDRIGE PROCESS, THERE ARE WINNERS AND THERE ARE LEARNERS.
—KATHLEEN HERALD-MARLOWE, CHAIRPERSON, 1999-2000 PANEL OF JUDGES, BALDRIGE NATIONAL QUALITY PROGRAM

Why adopt the Baldrige criteria as your route to organizational improvement? Let us offer three compelling reasons.

First, when you're seriously considering a quality improvement initiative for your school district, you want more than just another process to impose on yourself and your staff.

One of the key characteristics of the Baldrige framework is that it is *results-oriented.* It is set up on a point system; of the 1000 possible points, 450 are assigned to Category 7, Organizational Performance Results. Six areas of results are specified:

1. Student learning results
2. Student and stakeholder satisfaction results
3. Budgetary and financial results
4. Faculty and staff results
5. Organizational effectiveness results.
6. Governance and social responsibility results.

With Baldrige, you benchmark these critical areas, then continuously measure your progress toward the *results* you hope to achieve.

Another important characteristic is that the Baldrige criteria are *nonprescriptive*. Although they specify what areas you should be focusing on, they never tell you what to do. You know your organization best, and these criteria acknowledge and respect your expertise. They require you to think about aligning your organization to achieve results in these areas, but they don't tell you how to go about it. You have to design that yourself.

Finally, the Baldrige framework provides a comprehensive *description of an effective system/organization*. The criteria are based on world-class management practices, and they provide a framework for driving performance excellence through organizations already perceived to be high performing—like yours and ours!

The Baldrige framework is a great tool for organizational leaders when it is necessary to realign the organization to improve results and to accomplish your mission.

Tackling the Challenge

Leading organizations to greatness is difficult stuff. If it were easy, every organization would be excellent and, as we all know, few are. But if you are up to the challenge, there's nothing better to help you move forward than the Baldrige criteria. Baldrige has a long history of helping organizations move from good to great.

However, applying the Baldrige criteria to your organization isn't easy. It's not a one-size-fits-all patch for fixing problem areas. Adopting the Baldrige criteria for your organization may seem like a simple decision on the surface, but we're here to tell you that it's not! Propelling an organization forward in a logical, consistent way, meeting predetermined goals and objectives along the way, takes determination, commitment—and even guts! At times the process will seem infuriatingly slow; other times, it will rocket ahead so rapidly that you'll wonder where you lost control.

You have to be serious about it, make a real commitment to it. You can't have a casual relationship with Baldrige. Applying these criteria requires a new way of thinking that is profoundly different for most educational organizations. The Baldrige criteria have the capacity to alter at a very basic level the way schools are organized and managed. For example, working ceaselessly to better meet customer needs and expectations is a transforming concept for most school districts. In fact, even the idea of having and serving "customers" is a radical new perspective in the field of education.

Here are some things we discovered when we began the process of applying the Baldrige criteria to our school district:

- To use Baldrige effectively, you have to study the criteria intensely and discuss them constantly.
- You have to understand that the Baldrige framework is a means to an end and not the end itself.
- You need to know that most people do not naturally get excited or energized by the Baldrige criteria.
- It's a real copper-bottomed investment in your organization.

In 1761, the British Royal Navy introduced the practice of sheathing the hulls of ships with copper to prevent sea worms from eating into the planks beneath the waterline. The term *copper-bottomed* has come to mean an investment that is strong and secure.

—*When a Loose Cannon Flogs a Dead Horse There's the Devil to Pay*, p. 65

You'll encounter a lot of skepticism—and occasionally even downright resistance—from your customers ... maybe even from some of your most important customers: a school board member, a school principal, or an outspoken parent or community member. You'll have to be determined, even forceful, to keep the process on course.

Some of our teachers, for example, were quite candid about their feelings on this topic. They told us things like this:

> ... *teachers are being asked to do too many non-teaching/learning-related tasks. These take away from what we say is our mission. I don't think we have figured out what works best for us in the business-school Baldrige hierarchy .... Give teachers the training and time to absorb and use new ideas before putting a multitude of new ones on their plates.*

Too much time and attention are given to the latest 'gimmicks,' such as Baldrige and quality tools. They have their place, but we are spending too much time and effort trying to learn them. The tail is wagging the dog.

I resent that quality tools, PDSA, for example, are being stuffed down our throats. We are being forced to implement these strategies, whether we buy into them or not.

Also, the Baldrige process itself is labor intensive. It involves extensive and intensive assessment of where your organization is and where you want it to go. It requires benchmarking and continuous measurement and documentation, and forces you to look at parts of your organization that you probably haven't paid much attention to before. Some of the discoveries you make will not be reassuring, and when you discover problem areas, they may not be easy to straighten out. It's a significant undertaking.

Is it worth all the effort? We are firm believers that it is. Application of the Baldrige criteria has changed our school district for the better, and we have the data to prove it. We are operating more efficiently in all areas, our student test scores have gone up, and our customer satisfaction scores from students, parents, and teachers have been continuously improving.

A View From the Outside

Part of the reason for our district's documented improvement is the "view from the outside" that we gain from the process. For the last several years, Community Consolidated School District 15 has written a state application to the Illinois-based Lincoln Foundation for Business Excellence. In 2002, we submitted our first Baldrige application, and we resubmitted in 2003. Writing these applications is demonstrably hard work, but the experience is invaluable because of the outside feedback you receive.

"A system cannot understand itself. The transformation requires a view from the outside."
—Dr. W. Edwards Deming[1]

In 1997, we submitted our first application to the Lincoln Foundation, which uses the Baldrige criteria to recognize organizations in Illinois that are successfully applying the

"DON'T GIVE UP THE SHIP." AFTER A SHORT, BUT BLOODY, BATTLE BETWEEN THE USS CHESAPEAKE AND THE BRITISH FRIGATE HMS SHANNON IN 1813, THE CHESAPEAKE'S CAPTAIN REPORTEDLY DIED WITH HIS LAST COMMAND STILL ON HIS LIPS: "TELL THE MEN TO FIRE FASTER ... FIGHT 'TIL SHE SINKS, BOYS ... DON'T GIVE UP THE SHIP!"

—*WHEN A LOOSE CANNON FLOGS A DEAD HORSE THERE'S THE DEVIL TO PAY, P. 31*

principles of continuous quality improvement. We did win a Level I Lincoln Award for Excellence in Education, but the feedback report from the Lincoln Foundation was a startling wake-up call. We scored just 255 of a possible 1000 points, and the examiners identified 61 opportunities for improvement. It was disappointing, but we didn't give up the ship ... we kept going.

We immediately set to work on these 61 areas, and when we again submitted an application in 1999, we were viewed as being a better organization. In fact, that year we became the first and (still) only school district in the state to win the Illinois equivalent of the Baldrige award, the Lincoln Foundation Level III Award for Achievement of Excellence. We were very proud, but we still had more work to do. The Lincoln examiners awarded us 605 points of a possible 1000 this time, but they still identified 47 new opportunities for improvement. This feedback from the examiners, along with input from about 300 of our constituents in the community, helped us focus on other areas that needed work.

That kind of critical information is the key to continuous quality improvement. The feedback we've received from our first Baldrige application is forming the basis of our current improvement efforts. We're working hard to shore up those areas deemed to need more work.

We estimate the feedback reports we've received represent at least $50,000 each in consultant services. That's a great return on investment for the time it takes to write the application.

When all is said and done, you'll find that feedback is your friend. Sometimes, though, as we'll candidly admit, it's a very humbling friend!

Self-Assessment

The outside view is invaluable, but the view from the inside is equally important. The next step is self-assessment—using what you've learned to take an honest, penetrating, and comprehensive look at all aspects of your organizational operation.

Using the Baldrige criteria as a self-assessment tool allows you to measure your organizational performance against world-class management practices. You'll begin to see a clear connection between your education plan goals and the systematic approach embodied in the Baldrige criteria for improving organizational practices.

It's a good way to jump-start improvement initiatives.

How We Did It: Getting Started

The Malcolm Baldrige framework gave us an understanding of how our district could develop a results-driven, systemic approach to organizational improvement. We began by studying quality principles and tools and learning as much as we could about how other organizations were applying a quality approach to effect continuous improvement.

We opted not to create a quality task force or steering committee, but rather to work through existing leadership structures within the district. We reasoned that if quality were to become integral to all our activities, it should not be singled out as a special initiative; rather, it should simply be considered the way in which we do our jobs. Our administrative leadership team and the principals of our 19 schools would drive the initiative. This required a significant investment in training, so that all those who were to lead our continuous improvement initiative would know how to apply quality processes and understand what we expected to accomplish. Our leadership team quickly embraced the concept and enthusiastically set out to implement it throughout the organization.

We focused our efforts with the development of a new Strategic Vision 2005 (see the next chapter on strategic planning). This declaration created a clear mission and vision for the district: to produce world-class learners by building a connected learning community. In creating the plan, we sought out the opinions of more than 2000 of our customers to determine their expectations and what it would take to satisfy those expectations. The board of education then defined specific goals to support the achievement of the new strategic plan.

As we replaced what we now think of as a "tinkering mentality" with a core value of continuous improvement, we focused on another core value, management by fact. We began to measure everything important—in fact, we joke that our motto became, "If it moves, measure it!"

This was our starting point.

ENDNOTES

1. Deming, W. Edwards. 1994. *The new economics for industry, government, education*, 2nd edition. Cambridge, MA: The MIT Press.

3

Plotting Your Course: Strategic Planning and Development

In ancient times, brave (or some might say foolhardy) mariners set out for new worlds with only the vaguest of ideas about where they were heading. Their courage was remarkable, since in the early days of sailing, the only existing methods of navigation were notoriously unreliable, depending on visual sighting of stars and primitive methods of measurement. However, even had they known their destination, it would have been sheer luck to get there. Thousands of vessels perished in their attempts to navigate unknown waters, and even those that made it safely to land were never sure where they really were.

When District 15 began its journey to organizational excellence, we didn't fear falling off the edge of the world or being eaten by ferocious sea monsters, but we did feel that this difficult journey was too important to leave to the vagaries of chance. Fortunately, we had a clear idea of our destination, and we also understood that we needed a navigational system that could guide us safely from our comfortable home port of status quo to the exciting new destination we envisioned. Our navigational system—our Global Positioning System (GPS)—would be the Baldrige criteria. And our first step in determining our position so that we knew where we were going was to create a sound, well-crafted strategic plan.

Strategic planning is a popular topic in educational circles, as it is in business forums. It gets lots of lip service and media coverage. However, as we began to consider how to develop a strategic planning process that would guide our district, we couldn't find many examples of school districts

Global Positioning System (GPS) is a system of position and time measurement that determines position through triangulation between the user and four or more satellites.

It is used extensively in navigation as well as in many other scientific and commercial applications. It was originally designed jointly by the U.S. Navy and the U.S. Air Force to permit the determination of position and time for military troops and guided missiles.

with a strategic plan that was actually being used. Sure, we found some that sounded good, but we wanted more than just portentous-sounding words.

Baldrige says the strategic planning process should establish strategic objectives (or direction) and develop action plans for enhancing the organization's overall performance based on those objectives. The examples we found didn't clearly set objectives or direction, didn't plan actions, and made little or no connection to enhanced organizational performance. Obviously, a much different model was needed.

We did what Baldrige suggests, that is, benchmark organizations that have exemplary strategic planning processes. Baldrige winners are always a good choice, and so are examples that appear in credible books and other documents. The Web contains thousands of references to strategic planning models. A great source for best practice in strategic planning is the American Productivity and Quality Center (APQC). From the excellent examples we uncovered on this benchmarking search, we developed what we call our constituent-driven strategic visioning process.

The desired goal of this process was to determine what our constituents require and expect of students and the district, because the only reason we exist is to serve our constituents. In order to satisfy (and hopefully delight) them, we needed a clear picture of their needs and expectations.

The systems that support goal achievement cannot be improved if the objectives are not clearly aligned to our constituents' current and future requirements and expectations.

Once constituent expectations are defined, they can be translated into institutional performance requirements that, when taken together, become an effective management system. This management system includes:

- Plans for deployment of the strategic plan
- Integration of the strategic plan into school improvement and department plans
- Development and refinement of organizational processes to improve effectiveness
- Reduction of cycle times
- A process for evaluating and improving the planning and deployment process

In our district, we are fortunate to have a ready-made constituent group, the District Advisory Committee for Educational Excellence (DACEE). DACEE, which has been in existence since 1986, has 60 members including parents (PTA representatives from all of our 19 schools), both certified and noncertified school personnel, representatives of the district's board of education, union leadership, and community, business, and political leaders. DACEE's mission statement defines its responsibility: "To provide the superintendent with information about community perceptions and needs." The mission made DACEE a natural place to start. With superintendent and staff support, the committee began pulling at the oars, taking a critical leadership role in the strategic planning process.

PULLING AT ONE'S OARS MEANS TO HELP PROPEL THE VESSEL FORWARD BY DOING ONE'S SHARE IN THE COLLABORATIVE EFFORT OF ROWING. THE TERM HAS COME TO MEAN COLLABORATING ON ANY PROJECT OR ACTIVITY.

Planning for Our Plan

As with any enormous task, strategic planning is manageable only when approached in small steps. The first four phases of our strategic planning process built sequentially to accomplish the desired end result: an action-oriented strategic plan.

Phase I—Identify Key Constituents
DACEE members identify key constituent groups that must be part of the planning process. These include district staff, community members, regional, and state organizations.

Phase II—Identify Constituents' Requirements
District 15 Board of Education and senior leaders conduct community planning meetings and invitational focus groups to identify constituent requirements and expectations. This phase also quantifies the key external and internal factors, requirements, risks, and opportunities that define student and overall performance requirements. This information was tabulated by frequency and category counts and prioritized.

Self-assessment is a vital aspect of being able to develop a workable plan. We needed a clear understanding of where the organization was at that time as well as an honest evaluation of whether the district was truly capable of achieving a challenging strategic plan. We were fortunate to have in hand the feedback report from the Lincoln Foundation examiners reflecting the findings from our first application for a Lincoln Award. The examiners had identified 61 opportunities for improvement, and that was a good base line on which to build.

> **Phase III—District Level Self-Assessment**
> Senior leaders evaluate the results the district and its schools are currently producing in all areas of the organization. This phase identifies internal capabilities and needs, including assessment of student performance. External feed-back reports and category champion team (see Chapter 4) assessments are essential during this phase.

In a series of meetings, DACEE members discussed, debated, and eventually reached consensus that enabled them to hammer out the language that would crystallize their ideas and give the district an action plan from which to work. Once committed to paper, the document underwent extensive editing until, at last, everyone was satisfied that it accurately reflected the wishes and expectations of the district's constituents.

> **Phase IV—Identify Goals/Strategy**
> DACEE members, the district's board of education, and senior leaders identify key district and building goals/strategies that will produce results described in the requirements and expectations identified in Phase II.

Having worked our way through the first four phases of this process, we had our strategic plan. Because it was a five-year plan, we called it Strategic Vision 2005. The document spelled out the district's mission and vision, and defined our core values. Next, we convened board members and senior district leaders in a two-day workshop to align the board of education goals to that plan. We focused on six key goals and determined the specific strategies that would be the mainstay for those goals and help fulfill our mission/vision.

With our *Strategic Vision* in place, we were ready to map out the deployment phases of the process. Our first step was to communicate the plan to the entire staff and parent groups. We produced a video and distributed publications explaining the plan. A team of senior leaders went to each of our 19 schools to present the vision and mission and explain to staff

ASKING THE RIGHT QUESTIONS

THE INFORMATION-GATHERING PHASE OF OUR STRATEGIC PLANNING PROCESS POLLED MORE THAN 1500 CONSTITUENTS ABOUT THEIR EXPECTATIONS OF THE DISTRICT AND NEEDS FOR EDUCATING THEIR CHILDREN. SEVEN KEY QUESTIONS HELPED US DEVELOP A CLEAR PICTURE OF THE COMMUNITY'S VISION FOR THE DISTRICT:

- WHAT ISSUES WILL SCHOOL DISTRICT 15 HAVE TO ADDRESS OVER THE NEXT FIVE YEARS TO CONTINUE PROVIDING THE HIGHEST QUALITY EDUCATION TO ITS STUDENTS?
- WHAT ARE THE MOST IMPORTANT SKILLS STUDENTS WILL NEED AS THEY LIVE AND WORK IN THE 21ST CENTURY?
- WHAT STANDARDS DO YOU USE TO EVALUATE THE QUALITY OF EDUCATION IN SCHOOL DISTRICT 15?
- WHAT EVIDENCE WOULD PERSUADE YOU THAT SCHOOL DISTRICT 15 STUDENTS RECEIVE A WORLD-CLASS EDUCATION?
- WHAT PRIORITIES SHOULD SCHOOL DISTRICT 15 USE IN THE DEVELOPMENT OF FINANCIAL PLANS AND FUTURE BUDGETS?
- AS A SCHOOL DISTRICT 15 CONSTITUENT, ARE YOU SATISFIED? IF YES, WHY? IF NO, WHY NOT?
- WHAT WOULD SCHOOL DISTRICT 15 HAVE TO DO TO DELIGHT YOU?

members and PTA groups what the plan would mean to the district. We appealed for their assistance in deploying the plan, for without their commitment, the mission and vision would just be words on paper.

Phase V—Deploy Plan
Senior leaders communicate constituent-driven strategic visioning process and introduce Strategic Vision 2005 to all District 15 staff and parent groups. Short- and long-term instructional and operational performance goals and strategies are also communicated.

Phase VI—Develop/Modify District Scorecard
Superintendent and cabinet (senior administrators) develop or modify the District Scorecard, a measurement tool that would allow us to track our progress. The scorecard was developed based on the key goals and strategies of the strategic plan.

And finally, confident that we had covered all the bases, we began to implement the strategic plan using a quality improvement approach.

Phase VII—Operational Definitions, Performance Plans, Improvement Cycles
Department directors develop or modify work unit operational definitions and plan-do-study-act (PDSA) improvement plans. School leaders develop or modify their school improvement plans (SIPs).

Making sure that our actions are aligned to key goals is assured by strategic plan phases VIII and IX. Bringing the strategic plan to life and responding to an ever-changing environment requires continual assessment, ongoing evaluation of the feedback we receive, and even occasional redirection. It is an ongoing exploration.

Phase VIII—Monitoring
Leadership team formally monitors deployment of the strategic plan throughout the year.

Phase IX—Regular Reviews
DACEE members annually review the strategic plan requirements, assumptions, the general educational environment, and ethical, societal, technological risks

Mainstay takes its name from rope or line that supports the main mast on a sailing ship. In everyday English, the term is used to mean the primary support.

Mission Statement

The mission of School District 15 is to produce world-class learners by building a connected learning community.

Our Core Values are:

- Student- and constituent-driven quality
- Public responsibility and citizenship
- Management by fact
- Continuous improvement and learning
- Results focus

Our Key Goals are:

- Students and the community acquire 21st century skills
- World-class achievement
- Connected learning community
- Caring, safe, and orderly learning environment
- High-performing staff
- Aligned and integrated management system

OUR KEY STRATEGIES ARE:

- APPLY BEST PROGRAMS AND PRACTICES
- USE BENCHMARKING
- USE THE PDSA CYCLE
- DO SELF-ASSESSMENTS USING THE BALDRIGE CRITERIA
- APPLY SHARED-DECISION MAKING
- MAINTAIN FISCAL INTEGRITY

and trends that may affect District 15, and identify program implications (see Figure 3.1).

Among the steps we take to be sure we're on the right course are these:

- The DACEE reviews the strategic plan each year and determines if any key constituents have changed their requirements/expectations of the district.
- The board of education requires a formal self-assessment of District 15 using the Baldrige criteria every two to three years (Board Goal 3—see Chapter 4, p. 25).
- Category champion teams do informal self-assessments when formal assessments are not taking place.
- Educational Data Warehouse (EDW) trend data (see Chapter 7), employee focus groups, and survey results are also used during the self-assessment phase.
- The district balanced scorecard is verified or revised based on the key goals/strategies of the strategic plan, and all department operational definitions are aligned to the district scorecard. The superintendent and responsible cabinet member review district scorecard results for data at the department level, or with the leadership team if the data are systemwide information.

All this leads to annual verification or revision of goals and strategies—or a revision of the strategic plan if necessary. This overall process creates an ongoing alignment between constituent needs, key goals, measurement systems, and department/school improvement plans.

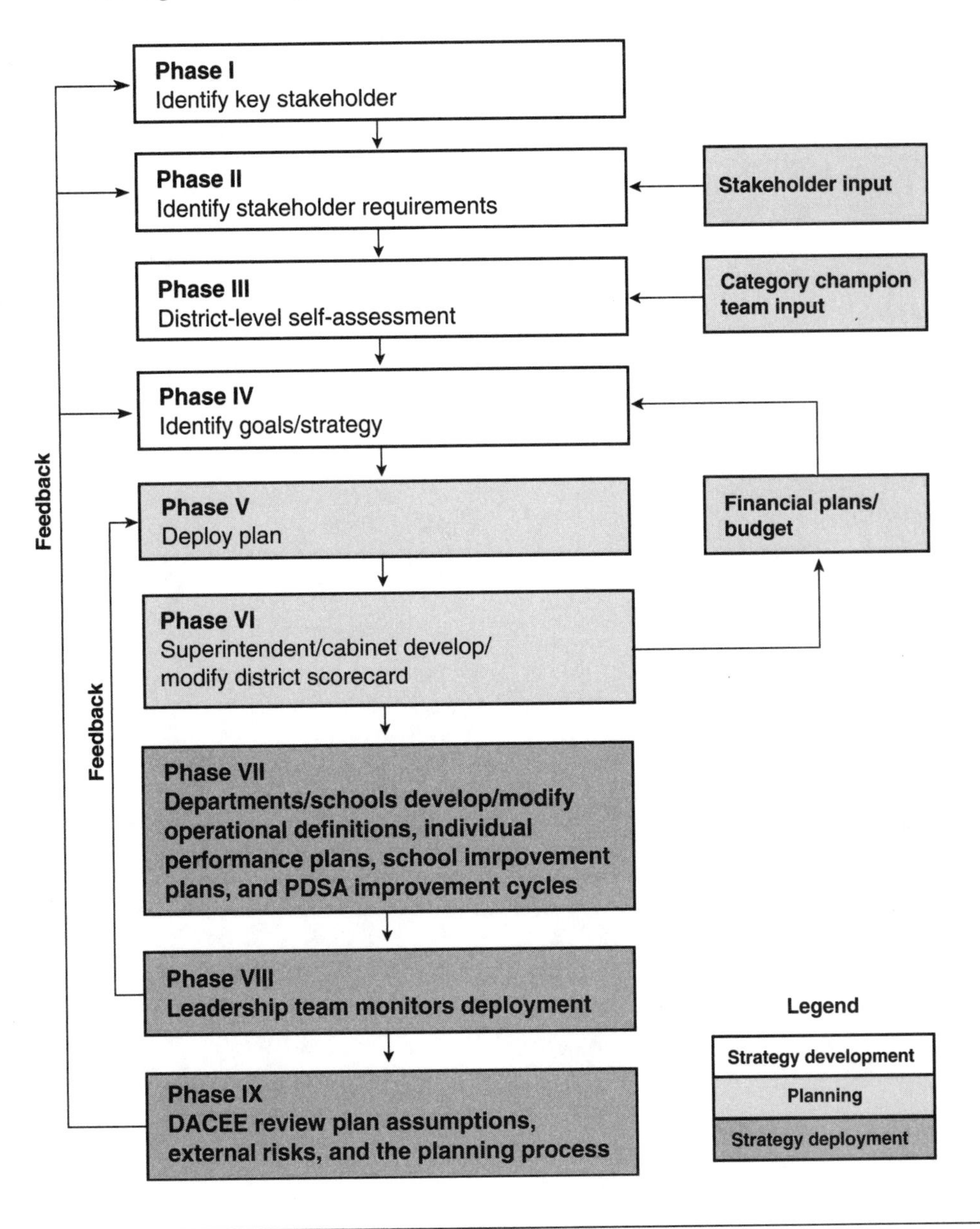

Figure 3.1 District 15's strategic planning process.

4

Precision Alignment: Aligning Your Goals to Achieve the Results You Want

Let's assume you are not pleased with some of the results you're currently getting. As a senior leader of the organization, it's your responsibility to define what the problem is. Are people lazy or incompetent? Aren't staff members motivated to improve or to meet or exceed goals? If not, why not? What do leaders do to find the causes of problems?

As many experts versed in the principles of continuous quality improvement have said, you can blame people—or you can blame the system. We subscribe to the Deming theory that almost all performance problems lie at the system level. People problems cause only a small proportion of the problems that affect organizational performance. Generally speaking, almost everyone in the organization truly wants to do his or her best—it's human nature to grab a problem and try to solve it.

To say this another way, the theories senior leaders are currently using in your district have created your current results. Their theories may be very good ones, based on lots of experience, knowledge, and in some cases, lots of pain. But, theories have to be applied in a framework that gives you a chance to succeed—and the Baldrige criteria make your theories about organizational improvement explicit.

Problems are usually created by misaligned (or in some cases, nonexistent) systems. Misaligned systems occur when people don't understand the organization's goals or directions, so they don't really know what they are expected to do. If they don't know where they're headed, it's hard for them

---

IN MY EXPERIENCE, MOST TROUBLES AND MOST POSSIBILITIES FOR IMPROVEMENT ADD UP TO PROPORTIONS SOMETHING LIKE THIS:

- 94 PERCENT BELONG TO THE SYSTEM
- 6 PERCENT ARE ATTRIBUTABLE TO SPECIAL CAUSES.

—W. EDWARDS DEMING[1]

97.5 PERCENT OF THE RESULTS VARIATION WAS CAUSED BY DISTRICT SYSTEMS, NOT PEOPLE.

—LEE JENKINS, FORMER SUPERINTENDENT, EDUCATOR, AUTHOR, CONSULTANT[2]

IF EMPLOYEES AREN'T MOTIVATED, THE FAULT IS WITH MANAGERS AND ORGANIZATIONAL PRACTICES, NOT THE EMPLOYEES!

—STEPHEN P. ROBBINS, BEST-SELLING MANAGEMENT AUTHOR[3]

I ALWAYS WONDERED WHY SOMEBODY DIDN'T DO SOMETHING ABOUT THAT. THEN I REALIZED I WAS SOMEBODY.

–LILY TOMLIN[4]

to stay motivated and maintain a good attitude and even harder for them to perform at an optimal level. When employees try to function in a misaligned system—even when they do their very best—all you get are random acts of improvement that can give an organization a false sense of accomplishment. Random acts of improvement happen in organizations more often than we would like to admit.

OK, so who's responsible for aligning the system? You are! Senior leaders are in charge of systems because they have perspective, positional power, and control resources. Next question: How to go about it?

Unfortunately, it is not easy to align systems—in fact, we found it to be one of the most difficult things to do. If it were easy, most organizations would be high performing, and most are not.

The goal of aligned acts of improvement is to have every employee to be in alignment so that what they do contributes to the accomplishment of the organization's mission. From our experience in tackling this issue, there are common barriers that make aligning an organization difficult.

The first and biggest problem in many organizations is the lack of a clear, measurable purpose or goals. A mission statement that is not measurable is a mission statement not worth having because you will never know if you have really accomplished it. To quote Harry and Schroeder, "Organizations that do not measure what they profess to value don't know much about what they value."[5] Believe that statement and it will serve you and your organization well.

The second barrier is a people problem. Aligning the organization will violate the comfort zone of many people. A recent article by Richard Elmore illustrates this point well. He argues: "With increased accountability, American schools and those who work in them are being asked to do something new—to engage in systematic, continuous improvement in the quality of the educational experience of students and to subject themselves to the discipline of measuring their success by the metric of students' academic performance. Most people who currently work in public schools weren't hired to do this work, nor have they been adequately prepared to do it either by their professional education or by their prior experience in schools."[6]

A recent statement we received from our teacher satisfaction survey is a good example. This teacher said, "Expectations are being raised every year. The emphasis on tests has grown every year. Perhaps parents and teachers need to say, 'Enough is enough.'"

There is a fear (or at least an uneasiness) out there that the process of aligning performance with goals will threaten the ability of individual employees to do their jobs in the way they think best. And in truth, it may. You have to be prepared for that.

> IT WAS THE RIGHT THING TO DO, BUT IT WAS PAINFUL.
>
> *—A DISTRICT 15 PROGRAM COORDINATOR QUOTED ABOUT AN IMPROVEMENT SHE MADE.*

The third barrier is that you need to decide how serious you are about aligning the organization because it's hard and because it will affect everyone, and some will not be happy about it. (See the first and second barriers.)

Now the good news. The Baldrige criteria describe what an aligned organization looks like. (To obtain a free copy of the *Baldrige National Quality Program Education Criteria for Performance Excellence*, go to www.quality.nist.gov where you will also find information on other Baldrige educational materials.)

Because Baldrige forces you to look at linkages between categories, the criteria give senior leaders the information they need to align systems. What we have found is that the Baldrige criteria are a valid and reliable assessment of how well your systems currently operate so you can focus your attention on the systems that are causing the greatest problems and improve them.

Educational organizations are a system of systems, hopefully all with the same mission. As Deming clearly states, senior leaders have the responsibility of optimizing the entire system, rather than the performance of individual parts.[7] To do that, you have to align customers, feedback, the aim of the organization, suppliers, input/output, and processes to manage the organization and continually improve (see Figure 4.1).

Two things are essential for any organization that wants to reach its targets—stability and accountability. We believe these are essential to align the organization so that it can reach its targeted goals.

Peter Senge and others wrote a book entitled *The Dance of Change*[8] in which he identified the challenges of initiating change. See if you have ever heard any of these:

- Where are we going?
- We don't have time for this stuff.
- This stuff isn't relevant.

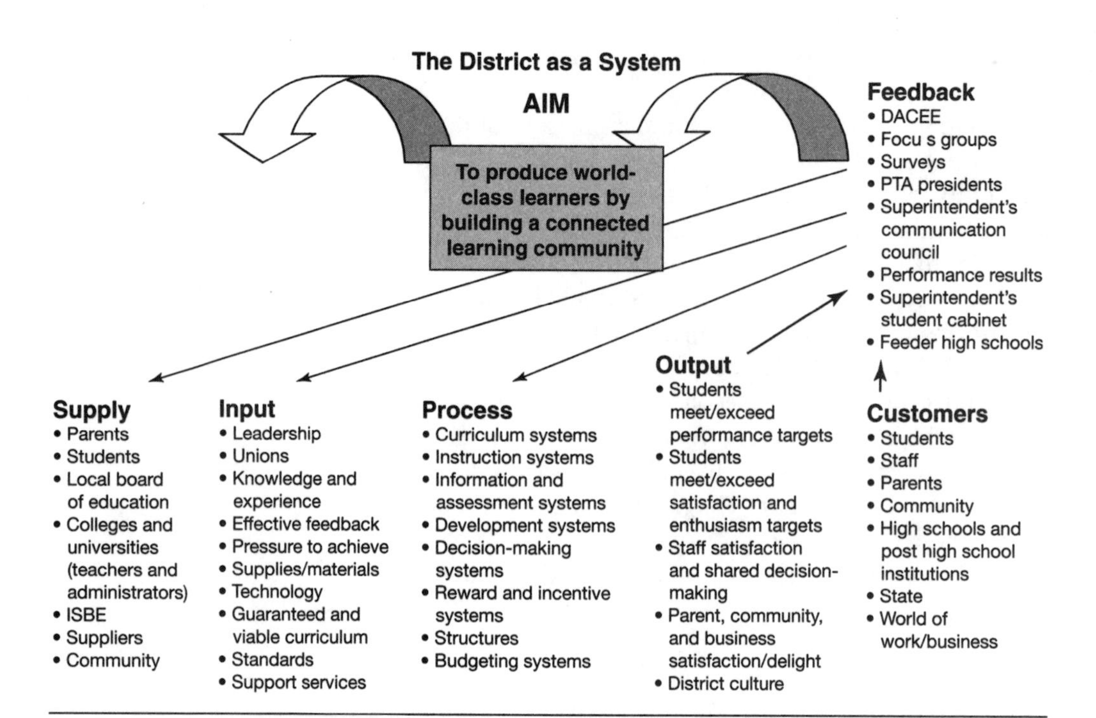

Figure 4.1 The district alignment plan.

- They don't understand us. We know the right way to do this.
- Who's in charge of this stuff?
- We keep reinventing the wheel.
- This stuff makes me feel overwhelmed and stressed out.

We heard them, and we're sure you will, too. You may not encounter all these challenges as you align your organization, but you will run into many of them. Senge suggests you figure out what set of forces in your organization may be working counter to your efforts (a force-field analysis), and then work with others to determine effective responses to deal with these challenges.

Developing the goals that will align your organization takes much input and thought. For our school district, it was a lengthy process that involved people at all levels of the community (see Chapter 3, Strategic Planning). The board of education established five key goals that would enable District 15 to fulfill its mission. What was as important as the content of those goals is that they were set up as five-year goals. That was a clear indication that the district's board of education meant business.

Having long-term goals means our schools and staff don't have to guess what direction we will be going in next year. It's dead reckoning—everyone knows where you are. There's no guessing as to how they will be held accountable next year. It means we can develop long-term plans for allocating resources and staff development. This is vital, because you simply cannot align a classroom, school, or district by changing goals, targets, your aim, or whatever you call your priorities every year. Holding everyone to very high goals is the right thing for a senior leader to do, but it is only fair to give everyone a realistic chance to achieve them.

It will also be necessary to confront what Collins, in his book, *Good to Great*,[9] calls "confronting the brutal facts." Employees know what's working and what isn't. They know because they have to work in systems that are aligned and in those that aren't. They know what's wrong, and in many cases, they know how to fix it. They want senior leaders who "tell it like it is." One superintendent recently stood before a large room full of his administrators from across the organization and said, "This is a good school district, but it is not a great school district, and I take full responsibility for this. I have let our priorities slip, but I am confident that we are now ready to move forward." It took great courage to say this, but in reality, this level of honesty is not risky because, as we said, everyone in the organization already knows it.

An equally difficult issue some senior leaders have to confront is the issue of organizational complacency. In our district it usually sounds something like, "We are good enough," or "We really don't need to get any better." Recently a staff member said, "Can't we just stop these improvement efforts for a while?"

Yes, continuous improvement takes time and energy, and yes, it means that things change all the time. And yes, we need to improve because all of our students are not meeting or exceeding our performance targets and that means some students are not going to have a bright future. If this profession was not so important to the future lives of all our students, then maybe a little organizational complacency could be tolerated. But it is, and every day is an opportunity to improve the educational lives of each and every student. They deserve nothing less from us.

BOARD OF EDUCATION GOALS 2000-2005

BOARD GOAL ONE:
INTEGRATE TECHNOLOGY ACROSS THE CURRICULUM, INCREASING STUDENT AND STAFF ACCESS AND USE OF TECHNOLOGY IN TASK-APPROPRIATE WAYS.

BOARD GOAL TWO:
ENSURE SCHOOL DISTRICT 15 STUDENTS MEET OR EXCEED STATE AND WORLD-CLASS PERFORMANCE STANDARDS.

BOARD GOAL THREE:
EXCEL AS AN ORGANIZATION, CONTINUALLY RAISING THE BENCHMARK IN ALL CATEGORIES OF THE MALCOLM BALDRIGE NATIONAL QUALITY AWARD.

BOARD GOAL FOUR:
BUILD A CONNECTED LEARNING COMMUNITY, BROADENING PRODUCTIVE PARTNERSHIPS AND SERVICES TO MEET THE NEEDS OF ALL STUDENTS.

BOARD GOAL FIVE:
BECOME A WORLD-CLASS EDUCATIONAL SYSTEM THAT MAINTAINS FISCAL INTEGRITY AND RESERVES AND PURSUES OUTSIDE FUNDING OPPORTUNITIES.

Using the information that a Baldrige self-assessment provides and having the courage to tell your staff the truth about how well (or poorly) the organization is functioning is a good start on the journey to organizational excellence.

Based on our experience, we recommend these four steps to senior leaders who are seeking to position (or align) their organizations for excellence:

Step 1

Ensure that senior leaders in the organization truly understand the Baldrige criteria. To apply the criteria effectively, a high-level understanding of the focus of each category and the linkages between categories is necessary. Senior leaders need to speak as one voice about what the Baldrige criteria are, why the district is using the criteria, the key characteristics of the criteria, and what they will do for the organization.

We brought our senior leaders together and developed what we call talking points—statements we would all use when discussing the Baldrige framework and criteria. A few examples include:

- Many states, school districts, and schools across the nation are getting astonishing student results and are touting the effectiveness of the proven Baldrige quality approach for organizational improvement. We know of no better way for us to achieve our goals than using the Baldrige criteria for continuous improvement in education.
- The purpose for using the Baldrige criteria is to build capacity to accelerate and sustain continuous improvement in student achievement and system performance. It is not about winning an award.
- The Baldrige criteria are simply a description of what excellent organizations do. In District 15, we use the criteria as a powerful internal and external self-assessment tool.
- By adopting the Baldrige criteria as the measure of organizational performance, we have also adopted the strategy of systems improvement. This means that when we find opportunities for improvement, the discussion and focus is about how we improve systems, not people.

Step 2

Have a clear and compelling mission/vision or purpose for the organization that has been developed by listening to the voice of your customer(s) or, as much quality improvement literature terms it, VOC. The strategic planning process described in Chapter 3 can be led by senior leaders to accomplish this necessary task. If you don't know where you are going, as they say, then you can take any path to get there. That is the definition of a random walk leading the organization nowhere. It is a leadership sin of the first order.

Step 3

Operationally define key goals that, if achieved, will guarantee that the organization accomplishes its mission. An operational definition, as we describe in the next chapter, identifies what needs and expectations the customer has and at what level those needs and expectations need to be met in order to satisfy, or even delight, that customer. A measure or measures need to be determined or designed that will help the owner of this process understand how well customer needs and expectations are being fulfilled, and a standardized data collection process needs to be developed so measurement bias or variation is not a problem (the old garbage in, garbage out issue). These operational definitions become goals or objectives to be incorporated into a scorecard used by senior leaders to monitor organization performance. District 15 uses the online One-Page Planning and Performance System, available commercially (for more information, go to www.onepagebusinessplan.com), to simplify this process and easily track performance over time. However, when deciding to use a scorecard, vision, mission, goals or objectives, and plans for improvement, you must align all of them with each other and with the district mission.

Step 4

Align job descriptions and work performance to the operational definitions. If the operational definitions are carefully designed, this will not be a problem because the definitions will clearly describe what people in the organization or function are held accountable for. This, for many, will be the most difficult step in aligning an organization, but it's probably the most important. You must have every staff member in the organization "on the same page" to achieve the operational definitions and accomplish the district mission. If the operational definitions are clearly stated, rewriting job descriptions and work performance requirements is not difficult, but it is time-consuming. The last part of this critical step is to assure that leaders and staff are evaluated on the basis of these job descriptions and work performance requirements and that rewards and incentives, individual and/or group, are also aligned to the descriptions and requirements.

These steps then help leaders apply continuous improvement practices at either the individual or department level. Figure 4.2 shows how this could happen.

Category Champion Teams

A strategy that we have used successfully for increasing ownership in the principles and practices of continuous improvement is the creation of Category Champion teams. These teams help assure alignment with the organization's mission, key goals, board goals, and related student performance targets. We adopted this process after benchmarking other Baldrige Award winners.

Category Champion teams are responsible for how the Baldrige criteria are applied within an individual category (see the following list), making sure resources are prioritized and distributed so that overall performance and student and stakeholder satisfaction improves.

Category Champion teams generally have at least two co-champions (co-chairs) and from seven to eleven team members, plus an advisor on call to the team. Team members help clarify what the criteria mean, determine approach and deployment, use data and documents already available within the organization to review and chart progress, translate the gap analysis into actionable improvements, and link across categories. Team members also suggest changes as a part of the continuous improvement process.

The Category Champion teams correspond with the seven Baldrige criteria categories. District 15 sought representation from all key stakeholder groups, so membership of each team includes representatives of the board of education, the teachers' union, principals, support staff, and the community (PTA). Each of the following teams is led by a senior leader (category champion) with support from the teachers' union executive board.

Category 1: Leadership
Category Champion: Superintendent

Category 2: Strategic Planning
Category Champion: Director of Planning
Membership: District Advisory Committee for Educational Excellence (DACEE)

Category 3: Student, Stakeholder, Market Focus
Category Champion: Director of Communications

Category 4: Information and Analysis
Category Champion: Director of Planning

Category 5: Faculty and Staff Focus
Category Champion: Assistant Superintendent for Personnel

Category 6: Process Management
Category Champion: Assistant Superintendent for Instruction

Category 7: Organizational Performance Results

Each category team 1-6 is responsible for the results of its own category.

Each team meets three times per year: we suggested that our teams meet in early November, January, and March. Teams allot three hours per meeting to adequately accomplish their agendas.

We developed a detailed month-by-month "to do" list for our teams (see Appendix A).

Telling the truth about current performance using information from Baldrige self-assessment, working on the four suggested steps, and convening Category Champion teams would be a bold start on your journey toward performance excellence.

The bottom line: Organizational alignment is the key to improved results. If you're a senior leader, check your pockets! You hold the key to your organization's success.

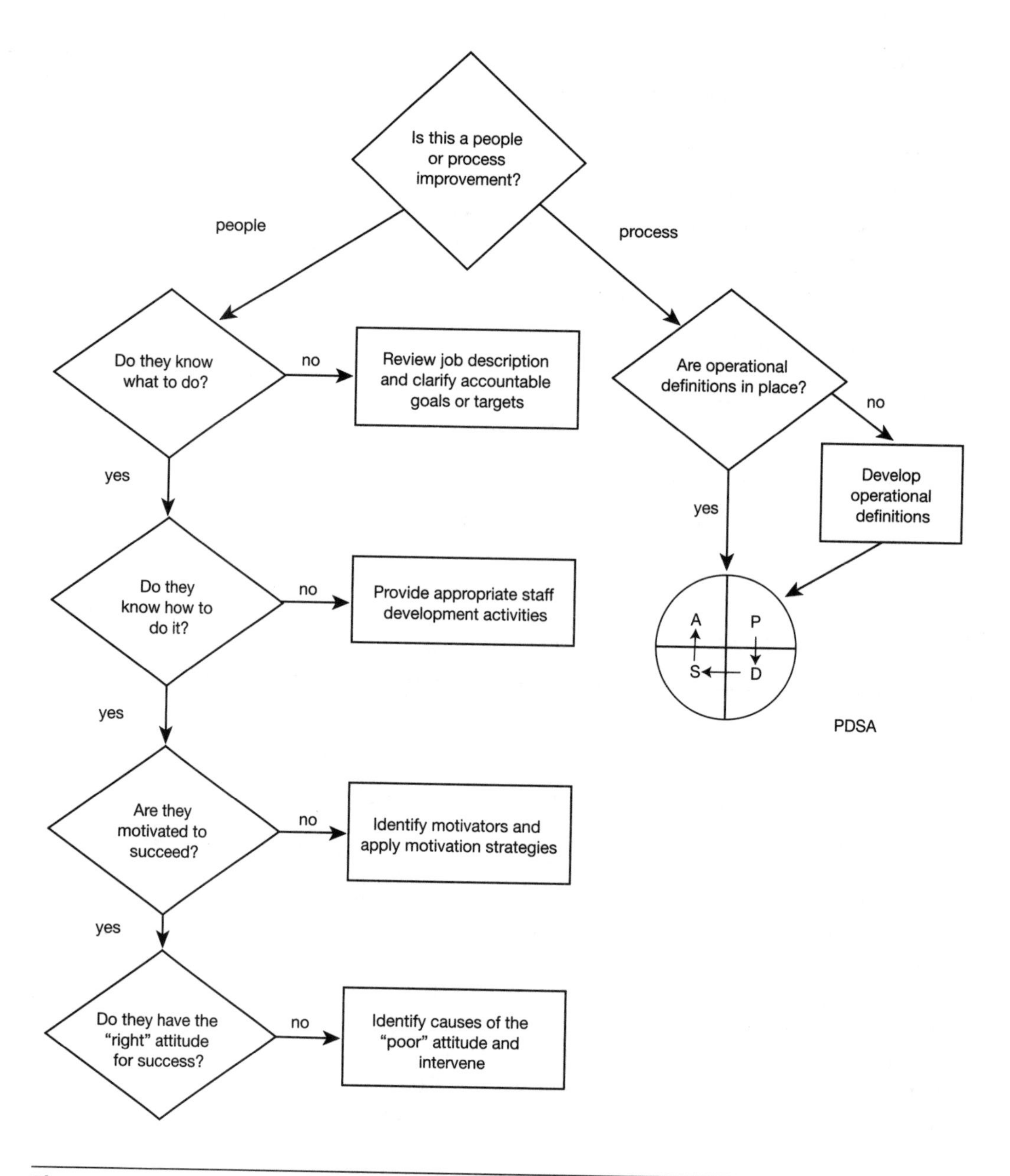

Figure 4.2 Decision flow chart.

ENDNOTES

1. W. Edwards Deming. 2000. (first published in 1994) *The new economics: For industry, government, education*, 2nd edition. Cambridge MA: The MIT Press.
2. Lee Jenkins. 2001. Presentation at American Society for Quality National Conference.
3. Stephen P. Robbins. 2002. *The truth about managing people ... and nothing but the truth.* Englewood Cliffs, NJ: Prentice Hall.
4. Lily Tomlin. A Lily Tomlin tribute site. See URL www.members.aol.com/nrb409/quote.html.
5. Harry, Mikel J. and Richard Schroeder. 2000. *Six Sigma: The breakthrough management strategy revolutionizing the world's top corporations.* New York: Doubleday.
6. Elmore, Richard. 2002. The price of accountability, *Results,* (November).
7. Deming, W. Edwards. 2000. *The new economics: For industry, government, education*, 2nd edition. Cambridge, MA: The MIT Press.
8. Senge, Peter. 1999. *The dance of change.* New York: Doubleday.
9. Collins, Jim. 2001. *Good to great: Why some companies make the leap and others don't.* New York: Harper Collins.

5

Aids to Precision Navigation: Your Balanced Scorecard

Assume for a moment that you are an assistant superintendent/director/coordinator of one of District 15's support services (curriculum, transportation, language arts, food service, mathematics, warehousing, nursing, and fine arts). In that role, you are the leader responsible for setting and implementing your department's improvement goals.

In the early fall of the school year, you receive a memo from the superintendent. It reads something like this:

> *Please plan to meet with me on (date) to discuss your department's improvement goals for the year and to review your plan, do, study, act (PDSA) improvement cycles. If your improvement cycle is not yet posted on our Intranet site, please bring a copy to the meeting. As in the previous year, I will be especially interested in improvements related to your operational definitions and your plans for benchmarking other organizations and practices.*
>
> *I look forward to our discussion. Our support services make significant contributions to the accomplishment of our district mission. This is your opportunity to share successes and lessons learned with other departments so that we can all benefit from your experiences in applying continuous improvement principles and practices.*

This memo demonstrates the significant shift that has occurred over the past few years in the job description of our

PRECISION NAVIGATION IS POSSIBLE ONLY WHEN YOU KNOW PRECISELY WHERE YOU ARE. ON A SAILBOAT, THAT MEANS KNOWING YOUR LONGITUDE AND LATITUDE. AS LEONARD EYGES EXPLAINS:

"ON ALMOST EVERY NAUTICAL CHART, THERE IS A SCALE OF NUMBERS ACROSS THE BOTTOM AND ANOTHER UP THE SIDE. THE BOTTOM, HORIZONTAL SCALE MEASURES *LONGITUDE* AND THE VERTICAL SIDE SCALE MEASURE *LATITUDE*. LATITUDE AND LONGITUDE READINGS ARE VERY IMPORTANT TO YOU AND THE COAST GUARD DURING AN SOS ... IF YOU EXPECT THEM TO FIND YOU."

–*THE PRACTICAL PILOT*, PP. 15-16

department leaders to include the responsibility of being a *process manager*. What does being a process manager entail? What are *operational definitions*, *benchmarking*, and *PDSA improvement plans*? How are department leaders supposed to use them to improve the quality of service to their department's various customers? What does all this have to do with a "balanced scorecard"—and what does that mean?

In this chapter, we'll offer some explanation and guidance.

Operational Definitions

To be effective, a support services leader/manager must have a clear understanding of who the "customers" are and why the service is needed. What service does the department deliver that its customers want? What is the expected level of quality for this service? District 15 approaches the answers to these questions by developing an operational definition for each support service.

An operational definition comprises four key elements:

- A customer requirement, or what we call the *quality characteristic*
- The *measuring instrument*
- The *method of measurement*
- The *decision criteria*

Let's explore each of these elements a bit more thoroughly.

Quality Characteristic

Notice that our approach to the development of operational definitions begins by understanding customer requirements/quality characteristics as *defined by the customers*. Our department leaders/managers don't just arbitrarily decide for their customers what the managers think they want or need, as administrators in school systems have often done in the past. We strive for a customer-oriented focus as clarified for us by this statement from W. Edwards Deming:

> *"Everybody here has a customer. And if he doesn't know who it is and what constitutes the needs of the customer ... then he does not understand his job."*[1]

Identifying who their customers are is the first step for our department leaders/managers. That task is usually self-evident, but the simple requirement of defining these groups or individuals precisely is a vital step in creating a truly customer-focused department. The exercise of identifying primary and secondary customers, whether internal or external, helps give a face and an identity to those who are being served and truly personalizes their needs.

This process does not have to be complicated. "What do you want?" is a simple question, and, in most cases, evokes simple answers. One warning though—the question must be asked in a sincere, "I really want to know the answer," way, and our experience shows that's not always common behavior. We all have a tendency to think we know what is best for our customers, and departmental managers and senior leaders are especially susceptible to this attitude. If they haven't asked their customers the "What do you want?" question or they haven't asked it in a way that elicits a valid answer, you have an example of organizational arrogance, intended or not.

Here's how some of our leaders/managers identified their customers and customer expectations. The coordinator of speech services sees her customers as students, parents, teachers, and building administrators. She finds out what they want through discussions at staff meetings and with administrators, at Individual Education Plan (IEP) staffings, by analyzing student satisfaction surveys, in student observations and discussion with teachers after observations, and by classifying e-mails and phone calls into categories of needs and wants.

Our director of literacy programs identifies her customers as classroom teachers, reading specialists, principals, program assistants, and parents. She learns what they want by gathering information from regularly scheduled meetings with teachers and reading specialists, teacher study group discussions, cluster (feeder schools) principal meetings, and e-mail and phone-call analysis, parent survey data, and the analysis of SIP goals.

The supervisor of food services knows her customers are students, parents, and federal, state, and local officials and inspectors. She identifies student wants by sitting with them during breakfast and lunch and discussing their reactions to the food being served. (She says their feedback is usually very candid.) She plans other informal meetings with students—what we could loosely call a focus group—to better understand what students want from a lunch program. She also initiates discussions with principals, her staff, and with officials during inspections. Parents get into the "wants" loop at PTA meetings and through phone calls.

As each leader/manager identifies the customers of his/her department and begins to quantify what it is that these customers want, you need to ask them an additional crucial question: "*How* do you know what they what?"

Our leaders/managers use a variety of informal and formal ways to determine customer requirements and expectations. We have found that face-to-face discussion between service provider and service user is the most effective approach, so we typically utilize focus groups, interviews, brainstorming, staff meetings, or leadership team dialogues. If broader input is needed, these discussions can be followed up by paper or group e-mail surveys.

The definition of quality characteristics requires listening to and learning from department customers. It isn't a complex process, but it does consume time. However, it is important because by identifying what your customers want, you can then identify what processes affect the quality of services provided to department customers.

IN MODERN NAVIGATION, A *FATHOMETER* IS A WAY OF MEASURING WATER DEPTH. THIS PRECISION INSTRUMENT OPERATES BY TRANSMITTING SOUND TOWARD THE BOTTOM OF A BODY OF WATER, THEN MEASURING THE ECHO RETURNING FROM THE BOTTOM. IN NAVIGATING THE BALDRIGE CRITERIA, YOUR MEASURING INSTRUMENTS WILL VARY DEPENDING ON WHAT YOU ARE MEASURING, BUT REGARDLESS OF WHAT "FATHOMETERS" YOU CHOOSE, THEY NEED TO BE RELIABLE AND PRECISE.

Measuring Instrument

The type of measuring instrument required is determined by the customer requirement/quality characteristic. Even though we call this an "instrument," it can include data-gathering approaches such as issue bins or telephone interviews, as well as such things as checklists, questionnaires, or surveys.

We keep a file of survey forms and other data collection processes gathered from other school districts, businesses, health care, and government organizations to help simplify and speed up the design of measurement instruments. We unabashedly borrow ideas when they seem appropriate to our needs, adapting and reworking the approaches that have been successfully used by others.

Good old common sense needs to prevail here so that instruments don't get so complex or burdensome that customers won't take time to fill out the form or respond to the request for information. (A word of caution: This is the first place in the operational definition process where poor choices or poor design will produce invalid information. The "garbage in, garbage out" axiom applies in the choice of measurement instruments.)

Method of Measurement
The method of measurement step shouts the word "consistency." It is essential that information be collected in the same way at the same time using the same instrument. If the method of data collection is not clearly described, you have just introduced another point at which your collected data can easily be invalidated. This is not the place for individual choice—there are plenty of opportunities for individual initiative in the final operational definition step.

Decision Criteria
The decision criterion is arguably the most difficult element of the process. What level of satisfaction needs to be attained to meet or exceed the customer's requirements? If the target is set too low, mediocrity creeps in. If it is too high, you lose credibility and those in the department who have to work toward achieving the target lose their motivation. The target has to be, as Goldilocks said when she snuggled comfortably into in Baby Bear's little bed, "just right." The "just right" target is one that will truly meet or exceed customer requirements and inspire your department staff members to continuously improve their processes to achieve it.

There is, of course, no single right criterion, but what helps enormously is getting comparable data or benchmarks. What targets have other organizations set related to similar customer requirements? You don't really know what good enough is until you have compared your targets with others. Wherever possible, it's helpful to make regional and national comparisons. We like to seek out Baldrige Award winners for our comparison targets so we know what the best organizations aspire to.

Putting Operational Definitions to Work...

We use operational definitions both districtwide and at the departmental level.

... At the District Level
On the district level, operational definitions—directly linked to the overall goals and mission of the district—allow us to determine how well our services are meeting or exceeding customer needs and expectations. They are key to helping monitor progress toward department excellence and to helping all staff members understand their contributions to

achieving the district mission. By clearly identifying operational definitions within departments and having measures that can be tracked over time, senior leaders can see at a glance how well the organization is progressing.

... At the Departmental Level

At the departmental level, operational definitions are used by our leaders/managers and their staffs to clearly define and measure the efficiency and/or effectiveness of the department processes for which they are responsible (see Table 5.1). These include such processes as on-time-delivery and safe operation of buses, the achievement of technology standards, curriculum development, network and e-mail reliability, staff development registration, school improvement plans, the safety of building and grounds, new food product introductions—and always, customer satisfaction.

... At the Employee Level

Operational definitions also apply at the individual employee level. We know that everyone contributes to helping move an organization from good to great, or as Charles Cobb says, "from quality to business excellence."[2] To reach a world-class standard of performance, everyone has to support everyone else. There can be no "weakest link" if you are truly trying to move your organization to a higher level of performance.

We regularly tell our senior leaders there are no excuses for not having clear definitions for what employees are held accountable for, how that accountability is measured, and for establishing standards of performance excellence. Without this information, it is unfair to judge the performance of staff members because they may not clearly understand the job expectations or the performance standards for which they will be held accountable.

The effort that goes into developing operational definitions pays off in some wonderful and unexpected ways. For example, the mission of our Custodial Services Department is to "provide a safe and healthy learning environment for all who enter our facilities. We are committed to continuous improvement and dedicated to quality." This mission supports one of the district's key goals: providing a caring, safe, and orderly learning environment.

A quality characteristic for our custodial staff is customer satisfaction. To measure customer satisfaction, custodians put a card on every teacher's desk two times a year.

Table 5.1 Examples 1 to 3.

Example 1—Department of Personnel and Human Services	
Quality characteristic	Satisfaction of the certified staff with their conditions of teaching.
Measuring instruments	• Monthly building-level staff meeting "Fast Feedback Form" • Focus groups • Annual districtwide "Conditions of Teaching" survey
Method of measurement	After each staff meeting, all professional staff members complete a "Fast Feedback Form" as an in-process measure to answer the question, "Overall, how satisfied are you with your job?" The forms are scored immediately after the meeting and analyzed for trends and opportunities for improvement. The data are shared with staff at the beginning of the next meeting and improvements are discussed. Focus groups of teachers are held two or three times each school year to collect staff satisfaction information. A person external to the district facilitates the discussion so that responses remain anonymous. Responses to the facilitated questions are recorded on newsprint so that focus group members can verify their accuracy. Comments are transcribed and posted on Learning Village, the district Intranet site. A more comprehensive Conditions of Teaching survey is designed to give us a districtwide assessment of certified staff satisfaction. Survey data (both quantitative and written comments) are collected in March at a school staff meeting. Surveys are given to the building union representative who turns them in to the district office for scoring. All comments are transcribed at the district to enhance autonomy. The surveys are tabulated by computer, and results are sent to each school and appropriate department for analysis.
Decision criterion	Meet or exceed benchmark (Baldrige winners) satisfaction standards of 90 percent. These trend data are used to determine what systems and practices that impact job satisfaction should be maintained, and what systems and practices show opportunities for improvement. Where opportunities for improvement are identified, benchmarking is conducted and PDSA action plans are developed.
Example 2—Transportation Department	
Quality characteristic	On-time bus pick-up and delivery.
Measuring instruments	• A check sheet designed for each school that identifies the route, the on-time delivery target, and a space to note if the bus is on time or late
Method of measurement	The check sheet is used for both regular and special routes, including special education, breakfast, and activity buses. The building assistant completes the check sheet for the morning and afternoon routes, alternating months between regular and special routes. On-time is defined as at or before the time of scheduled arrival. At the end of the day, each building assistant faxes the daily check sheet to the director of transportation and the percentage of on-time delivery of students is calculated.
Decision criterion	On-time delivery—98 percent or better. Data are scanned each day to determine whether any routes do not consistently meet on-time delivery targets. The director of transportation and staff determine the practices to be maintained and the practices that show opportunities for improvement. Benchmarking and PDSA action plans are the improvement strategies used.
Example 3—Department of Curriculum and Instruction	
Quality characteristic	Every student entering kindergarten will read at or above grade level when completing second grade. (This quality characteristic, developed to meet a key district goal for world-class achievement, is based on the belief that it is unconscionable to let kids fail first and then decide what should be done about it.)
Measuring instruments	• Second-grade Iowa Test of Basic Skills (ITBS) • Second-grade Acceleration in Literacy (SAIL) assessment • The Benchmark Text Assessment
Method of measurement	ITBS is administered in February. The SAIL end-of-program assessment is administered in May if the student did not reach the ITBS cut score. The Benchmark Text assessment is administered in May if the student did not reach the ITBS cut score and was also not in the SAIL program.
Decision criterion	Second-grade students will have a Normal Curve Equivalent (NCE) score in or above the fifth stanine or a SAIL end-of-program or Benchmark Text score at the instructional reading level for second grade. These data are both aggregated and disaggregated at the school and district level for analysis by principals and their staffs and the director of literacy programs and staff. Trend and disaggregated data are used to continuously improve programs and practices that impact the ability of students to read by the end of the second grade.

The card asks the teacher to rate the custodians' performance related to friendliness and courtesy, school cleanliness and maintenance, room cleanliness and maintenance, and school and service quality. The data are collected, aggregated, and returned to the custodial staff in each school for analysis.

One custodian noticed a one-tenth percent drop in his overall average from the first set of data to the second. He sat down and wrote a letter to the teaching staff explaining that he was very disappointed in this result, that he was going to find that tenth of a percent and earn it back, and he needed their help. To emphasize the idea of teamwork, he, along with other custodians in our district, designed a little card for teachers that said "Teamwork" on the front. Inside, it said, "Teamwork makes everyone's job easier. Thanks for keeping your classroom in mint condition." There was a place for the custodian to write the teacher name and a mint was taped to the other side of the card.

Needless to say, our earnest and dedicated friend "found" the tenth of a percent and more when the third round of data was reported. Now, we know that a tenth of a percent on a five-point scale represents random variation. But to this custodian, it represented a challenge to his professional pride and his ability to do the job.

This true story illustrates how operational definitions can successfully motivate staff to reach levels of performance they thought unachievable. It is an example of what can happen when meaningful performance targets are set and valid data are used to monitor that performance.

When we hosted a pizza party for the great results the custodians were achieving, we told them that they have been collecting and acting on some of the most impressive customer satisfaction data we have in the district. Since 1999, they have improved their overall average at every data collection point but one. Their customer satisfaction average is the highest of any of our district operations. And, we told them, we hoped they were proud of their mission, values, and key goals—because we sure were! They have demonstrated that mission statements and operational definitions are not empty words, but rather "the talk that they walked" every day in their schools.

... To Develop Measurements

A focus on operational definitions is important for another reason. It gives us a standard to measure. We believe the oft-repeated phrase: "You get what you measure," and its many variations, including:

> "Anything worth doing is worth measuring."
>
> "You can't manage what you can't measure."
>
> "If you don't measure it, you don't value it."
>
> "If you don't measure it, you can't improve it."

Working through operational definitions generates valid and reliable data—an absolute necessity for a senior leader. Taking regular soundings improves decision making by adding a measurable dimension to the "skipper's" combination of experience and "best guess." Because leaders/managers can trust its accuracy, the data that are collected can easily be turned into actionable strategies that drive rapid performance improvement on a 24/7 basis.

Once you've gathered your data, the customer responses need to be prioritized. An analysis process we've used successfully for this step (as well as much of the other qualitative data we collect) is to create an affinity diagram that organizes customer responses into categories, count the number of responses under each category, and develop a Pareto diagram to graph customer wants into priorities. The prioritized customer wants and expectations now become the department's *quality characteristics*, the first step in developing an operational definition (see Figure 5.1).

When you're satisfied that you have an accurate picture of the department's customer requirements, you're ready to ask a follow-up question even more important than the first: "Is your department meeting or exceeding customer wants and expectations?" That question is followed quickly by the equally important question: "How do you know?"

Obviously, what you want to hear is an informed analysis of customer data, not manager or staff opinion. As the old saying goes, "In God we trust, all others bring data." If a leader/manager has carefully developed quality characteristics for the department, this will not be an uncomfortable discussion. The underlying reason for asking this question is to find out if the senior leader or department manager is actually willing to respond to the wants and expectations of his or her customers. We have found a few instances where leaders thought just asking the "What do you want?" question was good enough. It's not. Once they've been asked, customers feel they have been

SKIPPER—NICKNAME FOR A CAPTAIN OF A VESSEL OR THE PERSON IN COMMAND OF A YACHT OR A SMALL CRAFT. THE WORD COMES FROM THE DUTCH *SCHIPPER*, WHICH IS DERIVED FROM *SCHIP* (SHIP). THE TERM "SKIPPER" IS FREQUENTLY APPLIED ASHORE TO A PERSON IN A POSITION OF LEADERSHIP OR AUTHORITY.

–WHEN A LOOSE CANNON FLOGS A DEAD HORSE THERE'S THE DEVIL TO PAY, P. 88

SOUNDINGS ARE A TECHNIQUE FOR DETERMINING THE DEPTH OF THE WATER. IN THE OLD DAYS, SAILORS TOOK SOUNDINGS USING A ROPE CALLED A LEAD-LINE, A ROD, OR A PLUMB BOB (WEIGHTED ROPE); MODERN SAILORS USE MORE SOPHISTICATED TECHNIQUES. IN YOUR JOURNEY TO ORGANIZATIONAL EXCELLENCE, YOU WILL NEED TO TAKE FREQUENT "SOUNDINGS" TO OBTAIN OBJECTIVE DATA TO GUIDE YOUR DECISIONS.

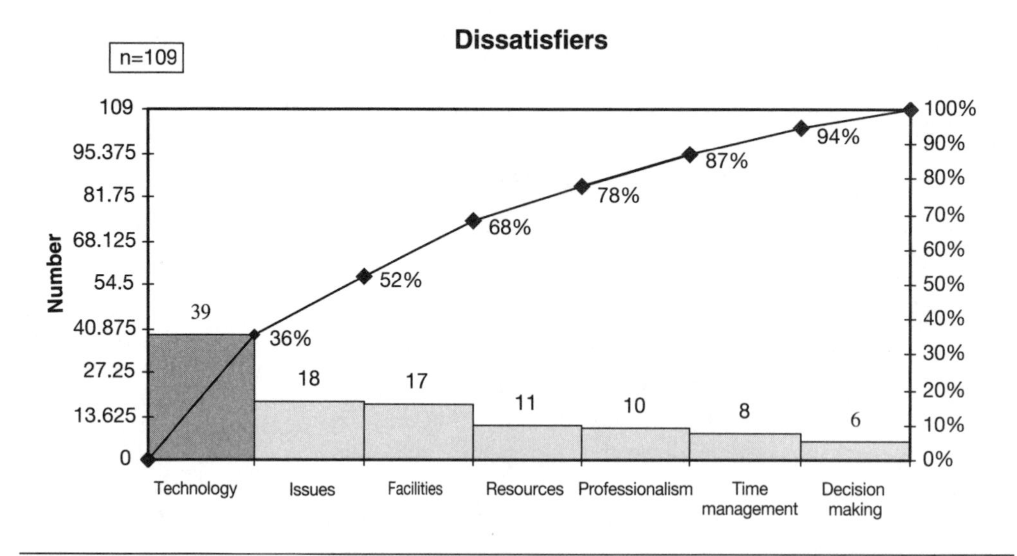

Figure 5.1 Categories of teacher satisfaction dissatisfiers identified using focus groups.

heard and that their opinions count. The department has to be reasonably willing to address customer expectations. Until you are confident that there is a valid and reliable set of trend data tracking customer satisfaction related to the quality characteristics, you do not have a continuous improvement process in place to address customer needs and wants. What you really have is a commitment problem—words but not action.

How you move words into action is through *process management.*

Process Management

The best description for this management concept we have found is by Leslie Steer:

> *"Every organization has processes, but many do not understand how the processes work, do not define them, and do not measure their performance. Processes define how work gets done, in what sequence, by whom, and to what requirements. (The customer's requirements, of course.) Taken to its logical conclusion, Process Management can be seen as the single overarching strategy for sustaining improvement and managing change. To be effective, process management implies* ownership of processes.*"*[3]

This definition requires leaders/managers to translate their customer requirements into processes they can map, describe, control, and improve—and then to understand that they are responsible for making sure these processes meet or exceed customer requirements.

Implied in this definition of process management is that, in order to meet or exceed customer requirements, processes need to be described and standardized. After all, you have to have a process in order to own it. We have confronted too many examples in our organization (and others) where managers talk about a process as though it exists, but when asked to describe the process graphically, cannot do so. Or, we talk about a process as though we agree about what it is, but when asked individually to describe it, everyone describes it differently. (See the discussion about our formative teacher evaluation process in Chapter 6 for an example of this phenomenon.) If that occurs, and we think it is highly likely that it might, congratulations! Knowing you don't have a process is the first step in developing one.

Developing a process is usually done by building a flowchart. When developing processes, we highly recommend Dianne Galloway's book entitled *Mapping Work Processes*[4] as an excellent resource for your managers to use as they work with their staffs to develop or refine processes.

For school district leaders, operational definitions and process management come together to form a scorecard of performance measures that determine the effectiveness of the organization.

Building a Balanced Scorecard

The concept of a "balanced scorecard" is usually attributed to Kaplan and Norton in work originally found in the January-February 1992 edition of the Harvard Business Review. They have since written a book entitled, *The Balanced Scorecard: Translating Strategy into Action*.[5] The concept itself is not complicated, but Kaplan and Norton suggest that while businesses routinely have measures in place to monitor financial process and results, there should also be measures related to customers, internal business processes, and learning and growth. A "scorecard" that incorporates these multiple measurements provides a more balanced and explicit picture of an organization's progress and opportunities for improvement.

A set of "balanced" measures as defined in Category 7 of the *2003 Education Criteria for Performance Excellence* can help school districts effectively monitor organizational performance (access www.quality.nist.gov for a downloadable version of the criteria). The category is described as a series of results that "examines your organization's performance and improvement in key areas—student learning results; student- and stakeholder-focused results; budgetary, financial, and market performance; faculty and staff results; operational performance; and governance and social responsibility."

This category asks for current levels and trends in student learning; student and stakeholder satisfaction and dissatisfaction; budgetary and financial performance; fiscal accountability; cost containment; work system performance; staff learning and development; faculty and staff well-being, satisfaction, and dissatisfaction; operational performance of key learning-centered processes; ethical behavior; and regulatory and legal compliance. It also asks for comparative results in each area.

This may seem like a lot to measure, and it also seems difficult to decide *how* to measure each of these result areas. If these areas haven't been measured until now, it is a lot and it is difficult, but if you work through one segment at a time, it doesn't have to be overwhelming.

Let's demonstrate how this concept of a balanced scorecard actually works in our district.

It's Tuesday afternoon and the superintendent's cabinet (senior leadership) is assembled for its weekly meeting. The agenda includes the usual topics—calendar updates, department updates, personnel issues, board meeting items, communication issues—along with a bolded item called the "One-Page Plan" with a name behind it. This bolded item has become one of the most important agenda items during the superintendent's cabinet meetings. Here's why.

Let's assume that the name attached to the One-Page Plan agenda item this afternoon is the director of planning. He (in our district this individual is male) has brought a computer with an LCD projector, or perhaps printed copies of his department's vision, mission, objectives, strategies, and action plans for review by the entire cabinet. The purpose of this review is to monitor progress in achieving this year's objectives and action plans. Cabinet members critique progress made on the department's objectives, which are aligned with the superintendent's objectives and with the key goals of the district as described in the strategic plan. This is where all that hard work to identify operational definitions comes together on a strategic level. The cabinet members will be looking especially for in-process measures (usually reported monthly or quarterly) that show the gap between actual results and forecast targets.

The director of planning begins his presentation by stating the vision of his department: "To be known as a world-class provider of comprehensive continuous improvement planning and deployment services to all departments and schools in the District 15 organization." The mission is described as providing the department's customers with the information, data, methods, training, and materials necessary to create the capacity for world-class performance. Notice a theme here. Our district's mission is: "To produce world-class learners by building a connected learning community." You can't produce world-class learners in an organization that itself isn't worldclass.

The superintendent and cabinet members nod their approval, then begin to ask the tough questions. "What do the data in your objectives tell us about how well you are accomplishing your vision and mission? How do you know you are a world-class provider of comprehensive continuous improvement planning and deployment services? With whom are you comparing your department's achievements? What is your progress in accomplishing your action plans and how do these plans support the accomplishment of your vision and mission?"

These questions reinforce the point that a vision and mission, no matter how inspiring or ambitious it may sound, will only be achieved by the hard work of designing and putting plans into action and demonstrating results by looking at data over time. We are not interested in words, we are interested in action, and that action had better be focused on and supporting the accomplishment of the district's mission. How well is the director of planning doing?

He says that his first objective is to increase the district from a band 3 to a band 5 Baldrige organization by May of 2003. (Bands correspond to descriptions associated with a numerical scoring range, for example, 351-455. There are eight scoring bands within the 1 to 1000 points possible.) He shows monthly data that begin at a 377 score in November when the district received its feedback report from the

Baldrige examiners, to 450 points in January, determined by a internal assessment. Extrapolating this trend, he draws a line to the 550 target at the end of May to show that continuing this rate of gain will lead to a band 5 organization by May of 2003.

Any cabinet member who wants to know how the data are being collected can ask to see a description of that process. Cabinet members offer perspectives and analyze progress to determine whether it is reasonable to expect that the objective will be achieved by the target date. A common follow-up to an analysis of the data about attaining objectives is to ask what action plans are in place to support the accomplishment of the objective. The director offers a brief description of each step that needs to be accomplished and the percent of the steps achieved to date. Again, cabinet members evaluate progress and offer suggestions that might possibly improve the action plan.

Each week a different cabinet member goes through a similar presentation and discussion. When all eight cabinet members have reported progress with their objectives and action plans, the agenda sequence begins again so that during the course of a school year, cabinet members will report at least quarterly. Also, because each cabinet member's One-Page Plan is posted on the Web, any cabinet member can access any other cabinet member's plan to get up-to-date information. If an action plan item is not updated each month, it is highlighted in yellow to indicate the need for immediate attention.

This regular, comprehensive review of individual cabinet member's objectives and action plans is designed both to help senior leaders in our organization by offering a broader perspective as well as to hold them accountable for their department's progress. It also serves to assist in the coordination of department initiatives. It is very useful to have other points of view enter the conversation to reinforce the director's analysis or to suggest a differing analysis. No one person knows the organization. It takes this kind of a discussion, focused on in-process data, to get a true perspective on the degree to which an objective will be achieved.

This new leadership system for reviewing and managing organizational performance was prompted by two opportunities for improvement noted in our 2002 Baldrige Feedback Report. One said that opportunities were not being provided for a regular review of key performance measures by senior leaders, which could make it difficult for them to assess success. The other pointed out that we needed a process to develop short- and longer-term action plans responsive to key changes in our services/programs, in our anticipated or planned student and stakeholder markets, and in our methods of operation.

The Baldrige examiners were right. We didn't have good systems in place to address this important management issue. Now, through the One-Page Plan process, we do.

As an example of the One-Page Planning process and its strategic use, let's look at how District 15 addressed one Baldrige criteria category.

In Category 7 of the Baldrige criteria, Organization Performance Results, District 15 established a set of measurable, quantifiable objectives. These performance measures become the district's "Balanced Scorecard" for assessing the progress of organizational improvement as well as for judging the leadership ability of key senior leaders.

Category 7 addresses "your organization's performance and improvement on key areas—student learning results; student- and stakeholder-focused results; budgetary, financial, and market performance; faculty and staff results; operational performance; and governance and social responsibility."

7.1 Student learning results

- Increase the percentage of all students achieving the 21st century skills (reasoning, problem solving, and critical thinking) from 50 to 80 by June of 2003
- Increase the percentage of second graders reading at grade level from 84 to 95 by May of 2003 for those students who have been in the district since kindergarten
- Increase the percentage of students that meet or exceed all state learning standards from 83.6 to 86 by May of 2003 for those students who have been in the district for one school year
- Decrease the number of subgroups that do not meet standards from 4 to 3 by June of 2003
- Increase achievement of students with disabilities from 53 to 57 by June of 2003

- Decrease the percentage of IEP students from 13.8 to 13 of student enrollment by June of 2003

7.2 Student- and stakeholder-focused results

- Increase the percentage of all students satisfied with their school from 77 to 80 by May of 2003
- Increase the percentage of all students who are enthused about learning from 65.8 to 78 by May of 2003
- Increase the percentage of parent satisfaction from 90 to 95 by June of 2003
- Increase the percentage of parents satisfied with special education services from 91 to 93 by May of 2003
- Decrease the student accident rate to less than 1 percent of student enrollment by June of 2003
- Decrease student bus conduct notices by 5 percent from 1234 to 1172 by June of 2003
- Increase student satisfaction with breakfast and lunch food quality from 70 to 80 by June of 2003

7.3 Budgetary, financial, and market results

- Receive the Meritorious Budget Award, the Certificate of Excellence, and the Government Finance Officers Award to certify fiscal integrity by June of 2003
- Reduce purchase order cycle time by 10 percent of a day by June of 2003
- Reduce the number of accounts payable checks by 3 percent issued on a monthly basis by June of 2003

7.4 Faculty and staff results

- Increase teacher satisfaction with their conditions of teaching from 78 percent to 85 percent by March of 2003

- Increase noncertified staff satisfaction with their working conditions from 85 percent to 90 percent by May of 2003
- Increase new teacher satisfaction with the induction/mentoring program from 89 percent to 92 percent
- Increase new employee satisfaction with the orientation program to 95 percent by May of 2003
- Increase the number of National Board Certified Teachers to at least two in every school by 2004

7.5 Organizational effectiveness results

- Increase organizational effectiveness from band 3 (351 to 450 points) to band 5 (551 to 650 points) by June of 2003
- Increase monthly SIP standardization from 25 to 38 by May of 2003
- Increase the number of school Baldrige self-assessment categories in the advanced phase for 27 to 50 by September of 2003
- Increase senior leader Education Data Warehouse utilization from beginning to competent by May of 2003
- increase transportation on-time delivery from 96 percent to 98 percent by June of 2003
- Decrease bus accidents to meet or exceed benchmark industry standards by June of 2003
- Increase network reliability to meet or exceed the 99.99 percent industry standard by June of 2003
- Decrease technology service cycle time to industry best-in-class standard by June of 2003
- Increase meals served versus enrollment by one percent by May of 2003
- Increase central distribution deliveries to a 96 percent satisfaction rate by June of 2003

If you are clear about your operational definitions, but are having difficulty reaching your targets or goals, the challenge is how to improve the system or process. We suggest the PDSA improvement cycle—a basic method for improvement used throughout the world. It is sometimes called the Deming cycle because it was W. Edwards Deming who developed the model in its current form and promoted it in Japan and the United States. As you will see in the next chapter, from the point of view of a senior leader within an organization, it is a proven way to manage change.

ENDNOTES

1. Deming, W. Edwards. 1993. *Public Sector Quality Report,* (December):.5.
2. Cobb, Charles G. 2003. *From quality to business excellence: A systems approach.* Milwaukee: ASQ Quality Press.
3. Steer, Leslie. "Process ownership: great concept, but what does it mean?" *The human element,* Spring 2001, Vol.18 No.2. Milwaukee: ASQ Human Development and Leadership Division.
4. Galloway, Dianne. 1994, *Mapping work processes,* Milwaukee: ASQ Quality Press.
5. Kaplan, Robert S. and David P. Norton. 1996. *The balanced scorecard: Translating strategy into action.* Cambridge, MA: Harvard Business School Press.

6

Nautical Charts: Your Guide to Preserving the Best and Improving the Rest

NAUTICAL CHARTS ARE ESSENTIAL FOR SKIPPERS STEERING THEIR WAY INTO UNKNOWN WATERS. TO DETERMINE THE SAFEST AND MOST DIRECT ROUTE TO A GIVEN DESTINATION, A SKIPPER MUST KNOW WHAT LIES AHEAD. AS CHARLES F. CHAPMAN NOTES IN HIS BOOK, *PILOTING*, "THIS INFORMATION CAN ONLY BE DETERMINED FROM CHARTS, ONE OF THE MOST ESSENTIAL AND IMPORTANT ITEMS OF EQUIPMENT FOR PILOTING A BOAT...THE SKIPPER MUST NOT ONLY HAVE THE REQUIRED CHARTS; HE MUST KNOW HOW TO USE THEM."

–*PILOTING, SEAMANSHIP AND SMALL BOAT HANDLING*, P. 336

If you do a Google search on the Web using the words "change strategies," you will come up with about 3,460,000 hits. Try "change processes" and you get 3,930,000. If you use "change management" for your search, you get 5,480,000 hits. There is even an International Center for Educational Change located on the Web, demonstrating the broad interest educators have in this topic. Recently, IBM has allocated considerable resources to the development of the IBM Reinventing Education Change Toolkit based on the work of Rosabeth Moss Kanter and found on the Web at www.reinventingeducation.org.[1] Robust models have been in existence for years—for example, the Concerns-Based Adoption Model (CBAM) identifies and assesses seven stages of concern individuals experience when going through a change process.

You may be asking, "Why, when this magnitude of resources on the subject is available, we do such a poor job of making changes?" After all, the history of education has shown that most interventions do not make a difference—not because they aren't good interventions, but because they don't get implemented.

Let's look at just one example. Principals in a large suburban school district, after being introduced to *What Works in Schools: Translating Research into Action* instructional strategies written by Robert Marzano, were asked what percentage of the strategies are currently used by teachers as part of their instruction to students.[2] Their consensus answer: about 50 percent. Now these are all instructional strategies (identifying similarities and differences, summarizing and note taking, reinforcing effort and providing recognition, homework and practice, nonlinguistic representations, cooperative learning, setting objectives and providing feedback, generating and testing hypotheses, and questions, cues, and advance organizers) that one would assume teachers would have learned during their undergraduate studies and be able to put to use during all kinds of instruction with students. This district is one where the teaching staff has an average of 17 years of experience, where the district provides multiple opportunities for teachers to stay professionally current, and which has approximately 2000 applicants to for every staff vacancy. Granted, this is a subjective assessment, but by school principals who should know what instructional strategies their teachers are using. This underwhelming assessment further illustrates the problems associated with creating and managing changes that make a difference.

Few subjects have been researched and discussed more than change. Yet, there are few good examples where change has been managed in an effective way that serves to bring about large-scale improvements. Ronald C. Brady's, *Can Failing Schools Be Fixed?* summarizes mild, moderate, and strong educational interventions across the nation over the past few years.[3] Brady points out: "It appears that no particular intervention strategy has a success rate higher than 50 percent, and most interventions yield positive results in less than half of the schools they touch. No one strategy can be counted upon to succeed in all contexts." Not a ringing endorsement for current intervention strategies, but equally important, we believe, is that much of that result has to do with the degree to which the interventions were implemented. The reasons are many, including ineffective staff development, teacher isolation, not providing time for the practice of new skills in appropriate contexts, the continual movement from one improvement goal to the next, and the lack of any meaningful incentives and consequences linked to skill improvement, to name a few.

Some observers are quite pessimistic about our ability to do much about this issue (see *The Predictable Failure of Educational Reform* by Seymour B. Sarason).[4] Others hold a much more optimistic outlook (see *Making Change Irresistible* by Ken Hultman).[5] A number of authors and editors have synthesized this body of work, few better than *Schools That Learn* by Peter Senge and others.[6] But back to our original question: With all these resources, the question remains: Why is it so seemly difficult to manage and implement change?

There is a rescue plan close at hand—an 80-year-old proven change management cycle called the PDSA continuous improvement cycle. This cycle, attributable to Dr. Walter Shewhart, was developed in the 1920s and later made popular by W. Edwards Deming in his work with business leaders in Japan and the United States. It has been used successfully worldwide by organizations, including education, as a basic framework for organizing and managing an improvement project. The PDSA cycle can (and in our opinion, should) be used for any incremental improvement project, regardless of the size of the effort. This approach to planned change is just as appropriate for small-scale problem solving as it is to organizational redesign.

The Koalaty Kid PDSA training materials say it well:

- Change is not easy, but it is not mysterious. It can be described and managed.
- Planned change occurs through the integration of theory and practice.
- Planned change follows a four-step improvement process called Plan, Do, Study, and Act.[7]

Basically, the purpose of the "Plan" phase of PDSA is to carefully define the specific change you want to make and then create an improvement theory (the change) that you think will improve or solve the problem. The "Do" phase of the PDSA cycle is where you actually implement the improvement theory. This phase usually consists of the well-known and common "action plan." The purpose of the "Study" phase is to monitor the data being collected as you implement the improvement theory to see if the improvement is giving you the change you want. The last phase, "Act," is where you decide whether you like the results of your improvement theory and want to standardize it, or whether you think more improvement is needed—which means you will start the PDSA cycle all over again.

We aren't going to provide an elaborate description of PDSA in this book because there are excellent resources available to do that (see ASQ's Koalaty Kid program). What we are going to do is illustrate the many ways PDSA can be applied to what Baldrige examiners like to call "opportunities for improvement," and share some lessons we have learned about using the cycle.

We first introduced PDSA into our organization in the 1996-1997 school year using some corporate training materials. It was soon apparent this was not the right thing to do. We hadn't created a context for using PDSA, and the corporate materials were difficult for participants to identify with, especially the application examples.

We got on the right track the next school year when we sent a core team of administrators and teachers to a national Koalaty Kid conference to learn about this group's improvement process. After a very positive review, we started immediately to train a team of five, including an administrator and four teachers from three of our schools. The next year we trained nine school teams and the following year, the remaining seven schools. We would have liked to train all the schools' teams the same year, but time and resources did not allow us to achieve that ambitious goal.

We started the first year using ASQ Koalaty Kid trainers, who did an excellent job. At the same time we began the Koalaty Kid certification process to certify internal trainers to continue the work. The training did just what we wanted it to, which was to spearhead deployment of a standard, powerful, and effective change management process throughout the district.

However, training was not enough. District systems needed to be realigned to fit the PDSA improvement cycle model. We discovered that after our analysis of the Koalaty Kid training when we found it not to be giving us the result we anticipated. This wasn't due to the quality of the Koalaty Kid training, it was because after three years of using continuous improvement principles and practices, we still hadn't learned the lesson of systems alignment.

Here's where the power of the Baldrige criteria comes in. If you use Baldrige, you have to think about and assess how well your organization's systems are in alignment. We aligned the School Improvement Process to PDSA (see Chapter 8) and even developed a SIP on a single page, again using the PDSA cycle phases. That's when improvements started getting impressive.

During the 1998-1999 school year, we also trained all our directors and coordinators of support services in the PDSA process and began to ask for written PDSA plans for improvements they wanted to implement in their departments.

But old habits are hard to break. Even with the PDSA process now standardized throughout the district, at the beginning teams using the PDSA cycle tended not to use data during the Plan phase, but relied more on opinions about what the gap was between where they were and where they wanted to be. We had to make data more easily accessible and understandable before teams began constantly using data to identify performance gaps. (See Chapter 7 for an elaboration of how data were made accessible and understandable.)

The second bad tendency that showed up in the Plan phase was that improvement or goal teams wanted to skip the root-cause analysis step and move directly from identifying the problem to finding a solution. We can't list the number of times we saw school or department teams prepare elaborate displays of data and do a good job of gap analysis, then jump immediately into brainstorming solutions. Root-cause analysis, the step that is most critical to understanding why a gap exists, was neglected or barely addressed. Team members rushed toward possible solutions without fully considering the root causes, hoping that a trial- and-error approach would hit the target by chance. This tendency has caused an enormous waste of resources in our district and in other organizations across this nation. When you don't identify the root cause, you are trying to solve the symptoms of the problem, not its cause. And what you get when you don't do a root-cause analysis are usually solutions focused on improving the wrong things and causing the expenditure of precious financial resources in an ineffective way.

Avoiding identification of the root cause poses less risk. That's because root-cause analysis often exposes the cause to be deeply held beliefs and/or behaviors that have been practiced for years. Understanding the root cause can be painful, because you have to confront the possibility that current practices are getting you exactly what you don't want. Tools most often used by our department leaders to find root causes are the relations diagram, cause and effect diagram, and the Five Whys. An example of root-cause analysis using the Five Whys tool in special education might have this outcome:

1st Why: Why don't more special education students exit special education programs?

Answer: More students don't exit special education programs mainly because of ineffective instruction.

2nd Why: Why is this a cause for the original problem?
Answer: This is a cause for the original problem because teachers who teach special education students are mostly ineffective in setting realistic learning goals, in using ongoing assessments to monitor student progress, and in adjusting learning goals based in ongoing assessments.

3rd Why: Why is this a cause for the original problem?
Answer: This is a cause for the original problem because preservice education, in-service training, and supervision do not adequately train or monitor these teacher instructional strategies.

4th Why: Why is this a cause for the original problem?
Answer: This is the cause for the original problem because there is a lack of real accountability for effective instruction in special education programs.

5th Why: Why is this a cause for the original problem?
Answer: This is the cause for the original problem because there is confusion or inadequate understanding about what effective instruction looks like for special education students in different programs, and without an understanding about what effective instruction looks like, it is difficult for teachers to be accountable for something they don't understand—which makes it equally difficult to supervise and improve special education teachers.

Another example using the Five Whys approach to identify root cause for unacceptable performance by low socioeconomic students could easily look like this:

1st Why: Why is student performance predicted to a high degree by socioeconomic level?
Answer: Student performance is predicted to a high degree by socioeconomic level because we do not use instructional strategies that can overcome this variable in all classrooms.

2nd Why: Why is this a cause for the original problem?
Answer: This is a cause for the original problem because if instructional strategies that can overcome the socioeconomic effect aren't used in all classrooms, performance will not improve.

3rd Why: Why is this a cause for the original problem?
Answer: This is a cause for the original problem because teachers do not know what instructional strategies overcome the socioeconomic effect.

4th Why: Why is this a cause for the original problem?
Answer: This is a cause for the original problem because we have not identified or shared examples with teachers about which instructional strategies overcome the socioeconomic effect.

5th Why: Why is this cause for the original problem?
Answer: This is a cause for the original problem because we do not know which instructional strategies can overcome the socioeconomic effect, and if we don't know we can't teach or practice them.

Here is another variation on the same socioeconomic issue:

1st Why: Why is student performance predicted to a high degree by socioeconomic level?
Answer: Student performance is predicted to a high degree by socioeconomic level because there is a pervasive belief among our leadership and staff that there is nothing we can do to change this.

2nd Why: Why is this a cause for the original problem?
Answer: This is a cause for the original problem because beliefs are a powerful predictor of behavior. If we don't believe it can be done, we will not act as though it can be done.

3rd Why: Why is this a cause for the original problem?
Answer: This is a cause for the original problem because our beliefs about overcoming the socioeconomic effect developed when we saw little evidence in classrooms that it can be done. We have not seen or read about examples enough times to change our beliefs.

4th Why: Why is this a cause for the original problem?
Answer: This is a cause for the original problem because our beliefs have significantly reduced our efforts, research, and exploration of instructional strategies that can overcome the socioeconomic effect.

5th Why: Why is this a cause for the original problem?
Answer: This is a cause for the original problem because we are not being held responsible for reducing the socioeconomic performance gap and are motivated to research and explore other things that seem to be more urgent.

One last example, this time focused on the role of a senior leader in organizational improvement:

1st Why: Why has our performance not improved significantly over the past few years?
Answer: Our performance has not improved significantly over the past few years because we don't know how to manage continuous improvement projects.

2nd Why: Why is this a cause for the original problem?
Answer: This is a cause for the original problem because without the knowledge and skills to manage change successfully, we can't improve.

3rd Why: Why is this a cause for the original problem?
Answer: This is a cause for the original problem because we have not seen our roles as being successful change managers and have not sought out training or resources in how to manage continuous improvement projects.

4th Why: Why is this a cause for the original problem?
Answer: This is a cause for the original problem because we have been given no clear goals or improvement targets, so we don't know what to improve or by how much, and we therefore don't value the role of being a successful change manager.

5th Why: Why is this a cause for the original problem?
Answer: This is a cause for the original problem because without being aligned to clear goals or targets, we don't know what to hold ourselves accountable for, what we are rewarded for, or what we need to improve, and without that information we see no reason to change what we currently do and become better change managers.

These examples of root-cause analysis show that significant changes in beliefs and practices are necessary because, when it comes to student performance, it's usually poor teaching or leadership that are the symptoms, but not the cause, which, as we have said many times before, is usually systems and alignment issues. Paying close attention and tolerating the pain of identifying the root cause will create much better results and save time and money. Believe us, we know.

The third tendency that gets improvement teams into trouble when using the PDSA improvement cycle occurs in the Study phase. During this phase, the improvement team is supposed to study the results they are getting as they implement their improvement theory. This obviously requires looking at what is usually called formative or in-process data, measures you take along the way to see if you are getting closer or farther from your intended goal. The standard operating procedure in our district was to measure it in the beginning, sometimes, but certainly at the end of the year, using standardized measures, to judge its effectiveness. Very little attention was paid to in-process data. There were a number of complaints: "Why do we have to collect all this data?" and, "We have more important things to do than collect all this data." Shifting the focus from summative or results data to formative or in-process data was not easy, but absolutely necessary.

It's only logical that in the Study phase, you have something to study. You can clearly understand how important this phase is if the improvement theory the team chose isn't effective. Waiting until the end of the year to find out your improvement theory didn't work is a waste of time, energy, and resources. If the improvement theory is designed to improve some condition of students' academic or social life at school, and it doesn't work, the loss may be unrecoverable, the damage permanent. That's a terrible price for students to have to pay for our neglecting the Study phase of the PDSA cycle.

The Act phase is the time in the improvement cycle where district, department, or school leaders meet with their staff to analyze the Study phase data and determine if the improvement was so good that it should be standardized throughout the unit, if the improvement is good but it could be better so there's a need for a new PDSA cycle to improve on the improvement, or if the study results were not that impressive and the improvement needs to be abandoned or stopped. Most often, study results are at the level of improvement that is good but more improvement is necessary so the cycle repeats. The point of the Act phase is that it is the time in the improvement cycle where decisions are made about what to do next. Usually, this is a time for celebration and "job well done" praise by leaders and examples of how a powerfully effective change management strategy, PDSA, and hard work pay off for everyone.

The template on the next page is the one we use throughout the district to develop all improvement plans (see Figure 6.1). It comes directly from the PQ Systems material used by the Koalaty Kid program. The written descriptions found in each step (except the action plan in the Do phase) helped to clarify and simplify the process. Everyone in the district, starting with students in our elementary grades, understands and applies the PDSA cycle when improvements are needed. See Appendix A for some examples.

Embedded in the use of the PDSA improvement cycle is the necessity for knowing and using what we refer to in this book as "the statistical and managerial seven." Many of the tools (affinity diagram, flowchart, run chart, cause-and-effect diagram, force field analysis, Pareto diagram, scatter diagram, histogram, and so on) are familiar ones frequently used for facilitated team activities and for many other purposes. There are many resources that describe these quality tools (PQ Systems, others) in understandable language, usually with examples of their use. They aren't difficult to understand—just ask the first graders in our district who use them all the time.

We have found that understanding and using these quality tools makes an important difference between effective and less effective school principals and other leaders/managers. Schools and departments that know how to use these statistical and managerial quality tools demonstrate high staff satisfaction and shared decision-making results. Mastering the quality tools and using them effectively shows up in how well our leader/managers can get the results we all want.

Our trip down the continuous improvement path could have been much quicker without as many bumps along the way if we had known then what we know now. But now, after many fumbles and bumbles, we have finally gotten to the point where everyone knows that when we're looking for improvement, the way we do that is by using the PDSA cycle. That understanding is making big differences in the way we perform.

We need to create a clear distinction related to the PDSA improvement cycle and another improvement process, benchmarking, that we are going to introduce now. The PDSA cycle, we believe, is for incremental improvements to processes, but isn't as valuable when radical changes are needed (see Figure 6.2).

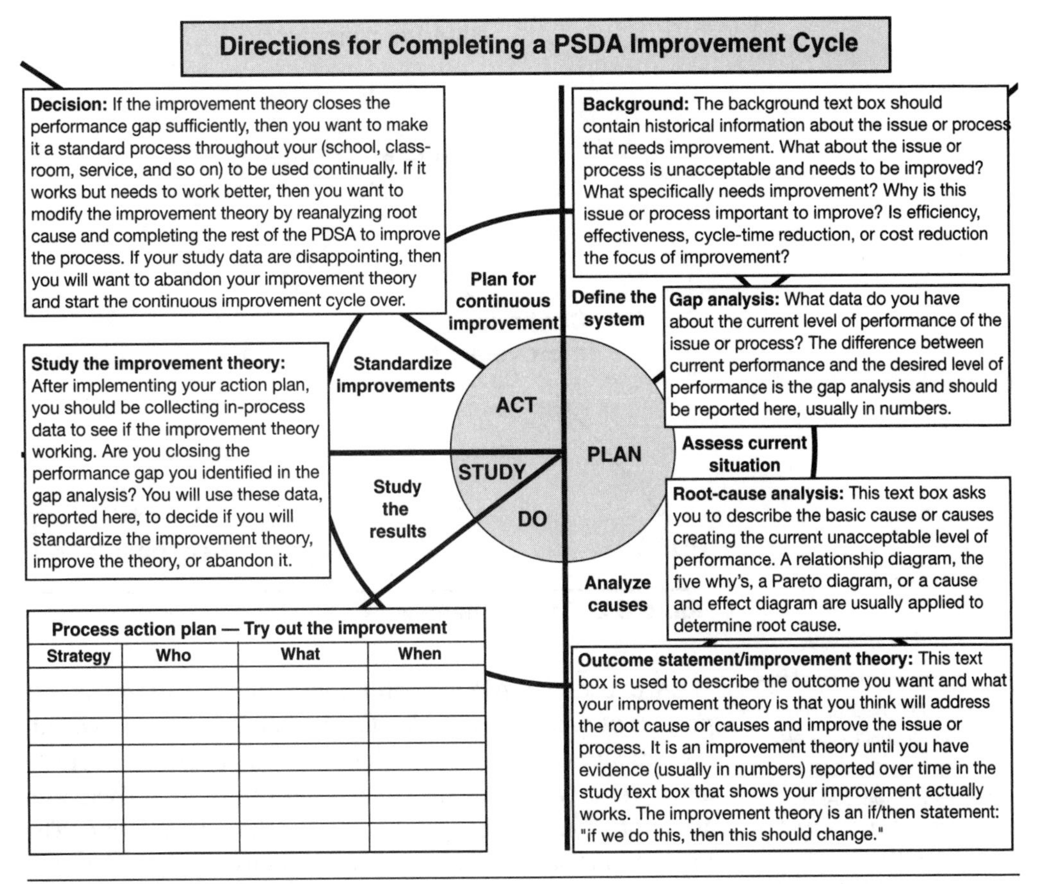

Figure 6.1 PDSA Improvement Cycle template.

For that we suggest the process of benchmarking. Coming up with a powerful enough improvement theory (the idea) to effect significant improvement is difficult when a *major* change to a program or process is necessary. Remember, we said in Chapter 4 that "all organizations are aligned to get the results they are currently getting." If people in the organization knew what to do to resolve the problem, they would do it, so it's likely to be a matter of not having the knowledge or skill to create the needed change. That's where benchmarking offers a better solution.

THE STATISTICAL SEVEN:

1. CAUSE-AND-EFFECT DIAGRAM
2. CHECK SHEET
3. CONTROL CHARTS (DON'T START WITH THESE)
4. HISTOGRAM
5. PARETO DIAGRAM
6. RUN CHART
7. SCATTER DIAGRAM

THE MANAGERIAL SEVEN:

1. AFFINITY DIAGRAM
2. ARROW DIAGRAM
3. DECISION MATRIX
4. FLOWCHART
5. FORCE-FIELD ANALYSIS
6. RELATIONS DIAGRAM
7. TREE DIAGRAM

Benchmarking

First let's make sure we are on the same page. Benchmarking is a process used to improve a process. A benchmark is a measurement or target, a goal to be achieved. The two words are often used interchangeably, but they are very different concepts.

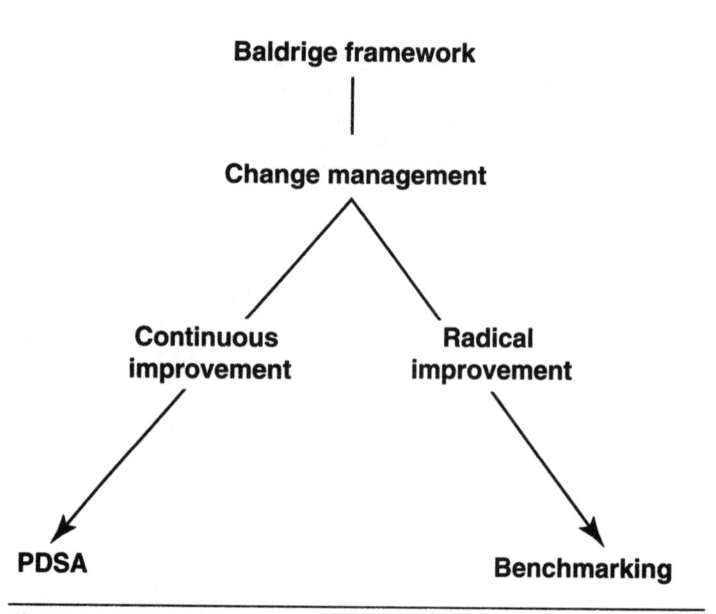

Figure 6.2 Baldrige framework.

THOUSANDS OF AIDS TO NAVIGATION—INCLUDING BEACONS, LIGHTS AND LIGHTHOUSES, BUOYS, FOG SIGNALS, AND ELECTRONIC SYSTEMS—MARK RIVERS AND CHANNELS FOR WATERCRAFT OF ALL SIZES. THE SKIPPER OF A BOAT OF ANY SIZE IS HIGHLY DEPENDENT ON AIDS TO NAVIGATION TO WARN OF UNSEEN UNDERWATER HAZARDS. THE SKIPPER MUST BE ABLE TO RECOGNIZE SUCH AIDS AND KNOW THEIR SIGNIFICANCE.

THE PDSA IMPROVEMENT CYCLE AND THE QUALITY TOOLS EMBEDDED IN IT WERE INVALUABLE AIDS TO NAVIGATION FOR DISTRICT 15'S JOURNEY INTO THE UNCHARTED WATERS WHERE WE WERE HEADED.

We use the APQC definition: "Benchmarking is the process of identifying, understanding, and adapting outstanding practices from organizations anywhere in the world to help your organization improve its performance."[8] There also are more "earthy" ways of saying the same thing. The International Benchmarking Clearinghouse thinks of benchmarking as "a practice of being humble enough to admit that someone else might be better at something and being wise enough to learn from them."[9] We like to paraphrase a more in-your-face description of benchmarking from Jack Welch, the successful retired CEO of General Electric: "Our school district should be the world's thirstiest pursuer of big ideas—from whatever their source—and we shouldn't be shy about adopting and adapting them. We should be well beyond this 'not-invented-here' stuff. We'll take ideas from anywhere, and use them as quickly as we can."

Why is benchmarking such a powerful practice? Look around at the best organizations in and outside of education, and you will find they use benchmarking and use it well. Benchmarking is one of the few management practices that has been validated as being a key driver for improvement. Ernst and Young and the American Quality Foundation conducted an extensive study that showed a statistical correlation between benchmarking and organizational performance, especially impacting both productivity and quality.[10] There are few other management strategies where you can find a statistical correlation between the practice and its result.

Benchmarking can be very helpful in "unfreezing" the apathy or status quo that keeps an organization stuck at *good enough* instead of *great*. It actively plays on the professional embarrassment that occurs when you watch someone else outperform you, not because they are more skilled than you, but because they have a better idea than you. Sharing expertise with others is the essence of benchmarking.

BENCHMARKING

A *BENCH MARK* IS A MARK CUT IN A STONE PIER, PILING, OR OTHER FIXED OBJECT, USUALLY IN THE FORM OF A HORIZONTAL LINE WITH AN ARROWHEAD SHOWING ITS MIDPOINT IN TIDAL OBSERVATIONS OR A LINE OF SURVEY.

—*ENCYCLOPEDIA OF NAUTICAL KNOWLEDGE*, P. 328

Let's take an example of how our district applied benchmarking to one of the most difficult processes in education, teacher evaluation. It was easy to identify that this process was in need of significant improvement. Teachers and administrators in our district told us the existing process wasn't adding value to the improvement of teaching or learning. Some were more blunt. They said the process was "worthless."

It was also clear that the process was not meeting our standards in terms of quality, timeliness, and cost. It was too costly and time consuming for the results it was achieving. Principals estimated spending between 6 and 12 hours per teacher to go through the traditional clinical-evaluation process. Teachers described it as a performance they staged for the principal twice a year.

In addition, the existing process was inconsistent with our goal of continuous quality improvement. If things are or aren't working, either way it is almost always the result of the system, not the person. So we asked ourselves, "How can we have a traditional teacher evaluation process while operating within the philosophy and practices of continuous quality improvement?" It was definitely time to revise the way we handled teacher evaluations. The process we chose to revise our evaluation process was benchmarking.

Motorola, the nation's first Baldrige Award winner (and a recent winner, too), a long-time proponent of continuous quality improvement, is a neighbor of District 15 and one of the many corporations with which we have developed working partnerships. We asked for Motorola's help and were invited to participate in two days of training on the benchmarking process. Motorola uses a methodology developed by Xerox, which has become the benchmarking standard used today by many corporations throughout the world. The model presents five phases a benchmarking project goes through to complete the process.

1. What to benchmark and what are the critical success factors to this process?
2. How do we currently do this process?
3. In relation to the critical success factors, who is best?
4. How do they do it?
5. What do we recommend to close the gap?

Step 1: Determined Critical Success Factors

We began the benchmarking process by understanding the characteristic, conditions, and factors that must be in place for the customers of the process—the teachers—to judge it a success. Identifying critical success factors is a necessary and very important first step in the benchmarking process that defines what we want to compare against best-in-class organizations. It helped us to focus on the issues that would make the most difference if improved.

The teacher evaluation committee members spent considerable time reviewing literature related to the topic, and individual members of the committee became "expert" in the content of the most important literature. Additionally, committee members discussed the strengths and weaknesses of the current process and asked their colleagues for the same kind of feedback. The literature review and extensive staff feedback about the teacher evaluation process led to a brainstorming session to create a prioritized list of critical success factors. Committee members agreed that the areas most important to the success of a districtwide teacher evaluation process were:

- Enhance instruction
- Encourage and promote professional growth
- Improve student achievement
- Ensure consistency of application across the district
- Provide clearly written directions and responsibilities
- Serve both formative and summative purposes
- Specify acceptable performance standards

- Use multiple sources and instances of data collection, including self-evaluation and reflection

These critical success factors were those key areas in which things must go right in the eyes of teachers if the process is to add value for them and for their students. They are also the factors that allow the district to distinguish itself as a superior organization where teachers have the opportunity to achieve a high level of professional satisfaction and growth.

Step 2: Clarify How Our Teachers Evaluation Process Currently Operates

We began this step by asking teachers to evaluate the current teacher evaluation process. Some of the more printable comments included:

> *"It isn't fair."*
>
> *"It doesn't encourage teachers to take risks or try new practices."*
>
> *"It creates fear rather than the desire to grow professionally."*
>
> *"It's not very useful in improving instruction."*

We called this information "frank and informative." Many of us thought it was also embarrassing to have a long-standing district process exposed, weakness by weakness, and think of how long we played this evaluation game with each other, knowing it wasn't working. Another humbling experience was asking our principals to flowchart the formative teacher evaluation process as it currently existed. Not one flowchart was the same. We had no process.

This meant that each principal had to develop an "as is" flowchart that came the closest to describing the current teacher evaluation process in his or her school—because without a flowchart of the process, we could not move ahead to Step 3 and identify critical success factors.

Step 3: Identify Who Is Best-in-Class Related to Critical Success Factors

One piece of advice: Do not approach this step by trying to find a single organization that is best-in-class related to all critical success factors. A quest for an all-around benchmarking partner is a misguided waste of time. Such a paragon simply does not exist.

Our committee used various sources of information (print, conferences, searches, word of mouth, and so on) to identify and select best-in-class candidates to benchmark. One criterion we used was to benchmark candidates from both the public and private sectors. We wanted to compare ourselves to best practices found in both public and private organizations throughout the world. Therefore, we considered information about private sector practices and negotiated initial agreements with private sector organizations we had chosen to be benchmark sites. At the end of this step, we had identified eight organizations for benchmarking, four school districts, three corporations, and the National Board for Professional Teaching Standards.

Step 4: Determine What Enables the Benchmarking Partner to Be Best-in-Class

"How do they do it?" That's, of course, what we wanted to find out. We divided the committee into teams to take the responsibility for determining the practices, processes, methods, and programs that enabled the partner to exhibit superior performance on the identified critical success factors. Each team:

- Developed a form and interview process for collecting data related to the pertinent critical success factors.
- Telephoned the site and established a contact person.
- Determined how the data collection will be done: conference call or site visit? (Every team except one used a conference call and found it to be a very acceptable way to collect information.)
- Exchanged agendas and any useful written documents before the conference call or site visit.
- Took the information the team gathered and determined what benchmarked practices would be feasible for adoption or adaptation to make our teacher evaluation process best-in-class.

By following these steps, each team gathered the necessary information so that the entire committee could make recommendations that addressed the critical success factors.

Step 5: What Do We Recommend to Close the Gap?
This last step in the benchmarking process required the committee to generate a list of recommended changes to close the gap between our current practices and our desired status in relation to the critical success factors. We also included statements about the expected impact of the change, approximate time for implementation, approximate cost of the improvement, and what major obstacles might get in the way of these improvements.

The result? The teacher appraisal plan we now have in place creates a climate that ensures quality instruction and enhances professional growth. It links instruction, supervision, and evaluation to staff development, and we believe, improves student achievement. It has also significantly enhanced the professional satisfaction of teachers in our district. We're proud to say that our process has now become a benchmark that other school districts have adapted.

Using benchmarking at the district level is a relatively easy sell because most administrators and department heads realize that, done well, it provides an outside perspective and uncovers useful process improvements. However, we've discovered that it is a harder sell at the school level where the "not-invented-here" attitude often predominates.

If you can't find an organization to benchmark that is exactly like yours (community, students, demographics, curriculum, and so on), all sorts of rationalizations for avoiding the process begin to emerge. We decided to bite the bullet and require each of our schools to make at least one benchmark visit to another school in our district. It proved to be the right bullet to bite. After the benchmarking experience, our schools found they had a lot to learn from each other—and they did. Practices have improved and professional respect has been heightened.

We have three observations about the benchmarking process:

1. Best practices abound in education, but we rarely know about them, don't inquire about them, don't share them, and don't adapt or adopt them. (The authors have had an ongoing argument/discussion about whether benchmarking is shamelessly

stealing ideas or honorably adopting them. Either way, it works.)

2. You have to be prepared to search for bench-marking partners. Finding them is often not easy, much less finding ones that are willing to cooperate. Some, in fact, were not cooperative at all and brushed us off when we asked if they would be willing to share practices with us. Just be prepared for that possibility and move on. There are many organizations that are very willing to participate in this process with you.

3. It's important not to skip any of the benchmarking steps … even though it is very tempting to want to speed up the process. If you do, we are convinced that the improvement(s) you wanted to see won't show up.

ENDNOTES

1. Kanter, Rosabeth Moss. 2001. *Evolve! Succeeding in the digital culture of tomorrow*. Cambridge, MA: Harvard Business School Press.
2. Marzano, Robert J. 2003. *What works in schools: Translating research into action*. Alexandria, VA: ASCD.
3. Brady, Ronald C. 2003, *Can failing schools be fixed?* Washington D.C.: Thomas B. Fordham Foundation.
4. Sarason, Seymor B. 1999. *The predictable failure of educational reform: Can we change course before it's too late?* San Francisco: Jossey-Bass.
5. Hultman, Ken. 1998. *Making change irresistible*. Palo Alto, CA: Davis-Black.
6. Senge, Peter. 2000. *Schools that learn: A fifth discipline fieldbook for educators, parents, and everyone who cares about education*. New York: Doubleday.
7. *ASQ Koalaty Kid Workbook*. 1996. Miamisburg, OH: PQ Systems Inc. and QIP, Inc.
8. *Benchmarking, benchmarking: Shared learnings for excellence*. 1997. Executive Summary, APQC Member meeting.
9. Kennedy, Eric, and Dan Rourke. *Once upon a benchmark*, Human Resource Planning, 16, no. 3:28.
10. ASQ, 1993. The International Quality Study Best Practices Report: An Analysis of Management Practices That Impact Performance (out of print).

7

Feedback: Reading the Tides and Currents

Across District 15, we have this tongue-in-cheek saying that "feedback is our friend." While that's a little glib, we actually mean it.

Feedback is always "a friend," but it doesn't always feel like it. When the Baldrige examiners bestowed 81 opportunities for improvement on us, it didn't seem very friendly, just overwhelming. When people in the community offer their sage wisdom and advice about how the district should be run, it seems overbearing. When you sit down to analyze student, staff, and parent survey results; student achievement data; financial information; committee feedback; and all the trend data in a One-Page Plan or a SIP, you may find yourself asking, "When is enough enough?"

NEVER MAKE A CALCULATION WITHOUT CONSCIOUSLY CONSIDERING ALL RELEVANT FACTORS: VARIATION, DEVIATION, TIDE AND CURRENT, LEEWAY (SIDE SLIPPAGE), THE SKILL OF THE HELMSMAN, THE EYESIGHT OF THE PERSON WHO TOOK THE BEARING, THE POSSIBILITY OF CONFUSION BETWEEN SIGHTED OBJECTS.

—*THE ANNAPOLIS BOOK OF SEAMANSHIP*, P. 242

Data are like any good thing, as well expressed by William Blake, "You never know how much is enough [feedback], until you have had too much."[1] We have, in many cases, become *data rich*—because we collect facts indiscriminately, and *information poor*—we can't learn anything from the data we have because the facts are scattered, unorganized, and not easily retrieved. Our data are stored in incompatible systems, like file drawers or even just in someone's memory, making it inaccessible to decision makers for analysis in a timely manner.

Educators can no longer afford to operate in this way. As decision makers, we simply must have the right information at the right time to be able to make the right decisions. If we don't, we have to base our decisions on our accumulated experience, opinions, and best guesses. When we are making decisions about the future of a generation of children, opinions and best guesses are just not good enough. This chapter will describe what we think enough is, why we collect the information we collect, and how that information is used throughout the district to inform the decision-making process.

We cited Jim Collins' book *Good to Great: Why Some Companies Make the Leap and Others Don't.*[2] In Chapter 4, the author bares his feelings about feedback when he says, "All good-to-great companies began the process of finding a path to greatness by confronting the brutal facts of their current reality." Those "brutal facts" are difficult to confront, even though you're not trying hide data or lacking in courage to face the reality of the situation. Generally, the more you disaggregate data, the more the brutal facts emerge. The good news is that by making feedback your friend, you are modeling the same behavior that moves good organizations to become great ones. The bad news is that it can get very uncomfortable looking at those brutal facts and holding yourself accountable for them.

In the Preface, we cited a mantra we use in the district: "If it moves, measure it." That may sound like contradictory advice when we're trying to answer the question about what enough is, but it makes a very important point about feedback. We promote this mantra for two reasons that are clearly articulated by Harry and Schroeder in their book *Six Sigma.*[3] The first is that, "If you don't measure it, you don't really value it." The second is, "If you don't measure it, you can't improve it."

For us, these were very disturbing statements because it was all too clear that, up to the time we read the book, we were practicing neither well. The statements imply, "regardless of what you tell me you value (all students can learn, all students will reach their potential, we value our employees, and so on), you don't really value these things unless you can show me how you are measuring that value." You may say you believe in the principles and practices of continuous quality improvement (and it seems as if everyone is saying that), but if you aren't measuring improvement efforts (and this means with in-process measures), you are not practicing what you preach. Look at what you measure. That tells people in the organization what you think is important.

It is easy to say we want feedback, but it is not easy to find the right performance measures to get the feedback we want. We encountered real difficulty in finding performance measures that aligned to our strategic plan, in part, because of a cultural value in education that complicates this issue. American education, according to Walberg, "is distinctively unaccountable compared with other aspects of American life and compared with education systems in other countries."[4] As we pointed out in Chapter 4, Richard Elmore says that traditionally there has not been a culture of accountability in education, and that even now, most educational organizations are not prepared to work toward accountability.[5]

Another reason for this cultural misalignment is that the Baldrige criteria can be described as having more of a strict rather than a loose approach to accountability. Frederick Hess labels this imaginary accountability continuum as coercive to suggestive.[6] Strict or coercive accountability would have incentives, sanctions, compensation, and evaluation tightly linked to achieving goals or meeting or exceeding results targets. It would have tests for passing a class or getting a diploma. It would be characterized by performance that is clearly and carefully measured. Loose or suggestive accountability, on the other hand, can be described by the use of informal social pressure, a single-scale or seniority-based salary schedule, personnel evaluation by criteria (classroom management, communication ability, teaching techniques, professional responsibilities, follows policy and procedures, and so on) or rubric (exceeds expectations, meets standards, excellent, satisfactory, unsatisfactory, and so on), and using the "we think" it's working well, or "we think" we're doing just fine approach to measuring performance. The problem is that education tends toward the loose or suggestive side of accountability, while almost all high performing organizations (public or private) are on the strict or coercive side of the accountability continuum.

If you don't yet believe those observations, you will as you continue to collect and push data into the organization. Management by fact creates a culture clash of major proportions, and as a senior leader in your organization, you end up in the middle of it, as you should. This is a cultural clash worth confronting and winning.

You win by recognizing and acknowledging that where there is blame (think brutal facts), it's the system that is to blame, not the people. Staff members are doing their best in a system that is not aligned or not purposeful. If the system is not aligned or purposeful, then staff cannot reach their full potential and will likely be less than motivated in their job.

GETTING TO THE BITTER END GENERALLY MEANS EXHAUSTING ALL OPTIONS AFTER A DIFFICULT STRUGGLE. IN NAUTICAL TERMS, IT'S THE INBOARD END OF AN ANCHOR ROPE. AS BILL BEAVIS AND RICHARD MCCLOSKEY EXPLAINED IN *SALTY DOG TALK*, "THE ANCHOR ROPE ON OLD SAILING VESSELS WAS ATTACHED TO A STOUT OAK POST CALLED A BITT, WHICH WAS FIRMLY FASTENED TO THE DECK. SECURING TURNS WERE TAKEN AROUND THE BITT AS ANCHOR AND ANCHOR ROPE WERE PAID OUT TO THE SEA ... WHEN AT THE END OF YOUR ROPE, ON LAND OR AT SEA, YOU'VE REACHED THE BITTER END."

But you haven't yet reached the bitter end. You can do something about alignment and purpose, and that is where your energy and commitment should be dedicated.

What to Collect?

If you want feedback, you need measures. Begin your search for measures with a strategic plan that clearly defines the aim or goals of the organization. Being a mission-driven organization isn't just nice to do, it's a necessity. Without an articulated direction for the organization to move toward, it's impossible to decide which measures will be useful and which won't.

The essence of our strategic plan is the mission statement on p. 19, Chapter 3. Our mission, core values, key goals, board goals, and our student performance targets are printed on a small pocket-sized brochure that we distribute liberally. We expect our staff to know the mission of the district, so all new employees are greeted with an orientation to the mission, what it means to an employee in the district, and how we measure our progress toward achievement of that mission. Employees are then able to directly link what they do to the accomplishment of our mission. That's important, because measures are just measures until they have personal meaning. If a staff member does not know why a measure is so important to his or her job performance, that employee will, logically, neglect it or find it irrelevant. Making these connections between measures and work performance is the job of a senior leader. The result is a motivated staff.

We explained in Chapter 2 how valuable Baldrige-based feedback reports have been to our organization. Here is an example. When we received the 1999 Feedback Report from the Lincoln Foundation for Business Excellence (the Lincoln award is the Illinois version of the Baldrige Award process and uses the same criteria, it listed 49 opportunities for improvement. Stuck among them was this little gem:

> *Current and future performance targets ... have not been translated into specific, measurable performance goals or comparable terms, beyond the state goals of 'gap reduction,' 'statistically significant increase,' 'reduction,' or 'decrease.' This could impact the district's*

ability to measure progress and achieve its stated objective of world-class performance.

There, stated succinctly, was a revolution that needed to happen. The key problem with our measurement system was that we didn't have measurable goals; therefore, we couldn't tell if our achievements were important.

During this same time, in one of our strategic planning sessions, district constituents told us they wanted District 15 to "produce world-class learners." A lovely, lofty-sounding goal, we thought. But our board of education asked the administration a pointed question: "What does world-class achievement mean?"

Those two things—the Lincoln Award feedback report's opportunity for improvement and the board question—transformed our thinking about goals and measures. In response, we began benchmarking what we determined were world-class school districts and carefully looking at their performance goals or targets. There was nothing new here, just a synthesis of the best ideas from the best organizations. The result: we developed specific, quantifiable Student Performance Targets to reflect our definition of world-class performance standards. These Student Performance Targets were adopted by the board of education in September 2000.

Notice the measurability of each Student Performance Target. We have operationally defined each target to identify a measuring instrument or instruments, defined the measurement process, and set a target. Notice also that these targets don't just say, "improve" or "increase." They specify a number. It took us quite a while to understand just how important this kind of specificity is in creating an organizational focus and alignment … and, it created a revolution! This was a cultural "shock" to district staff that took considerable senior leader time and energy to manage and overcome. Comments from our surveys like "get real" and "the standards in this district are way too high" were particularly disheartening. But even this negative feedback strengthened our resolve and made us confident that we were on the right track. Our experience has proved that setting high expectations and measurable targets is absolutely the right thing to do, and so is giving people in the organization the time to achieve them. This means we are all "on the same page." In our case, some pretty extraordinary things happened when we all got on the same page.

Student Performance Targets

- Students acquire the 21st century skills of:
  - Accessing and understanding information
  - Oral and written communication
  - Comprehensive reading and understanding
  - Reasoning, problem-solving, and critical thinking
  - Human relations
  - Life skills
- Every student entering kindergarten in District 15 reads at or above grade level when completing second grade.
- At least 90 percent of the students who have been in the district for one year meet or exceeds all Illinois Learning Standards.
- There is no significant difference between student groups in meeting or exceeding all Illinois Learning Standards for students who have been in the district for one year.
- Student satisfaction is at or above best-in-class benchmark standards.
- Student enthusiasm is at or above best-in-class benchmark standards.

THE STUDENT PERFORMANCE TARGETS ARE OUR *WAYPOINTS*. "WAYPOINTS" ARE INTERIM DESTINATIONS EN ROUTE TO A FINAL DESTINATION. MODERN SAILORS CAN SIMPLY CLICK THEIR TARGETED DESTINATION FROM ELECTRONIC CHARTS TO OBTAIN THE WAYPOINTS FOR THEIR JOURNEY.

With our Student Performance Targets, accountability is very clear. If you are a kindergarten, first-, or second-grade teacher, you know your most important task is to have students reading at or above grade level by the end of second grade. Central office support staff members know they are responsible for having programs and practices available to teachers that align to and support the accomplishment of that target. Principals monitor the reading target down to the individual student level. They know which students will achieve the target, who is "on the bubble," and who needs intensive help. They also know that their evaluation is directly aligned to the accomplishment of the Student Performance Targets.

Reporting and Analyzing Data Trends

Data trends from the Balanced Scorecard are used at all levels of the organization. Discussions between cabinet members and the superintendent focus on trend data being reported and on appropriate progress in meeting or exceeding target performance.

Cabinet members are responsible for communicating scorecard data trends to their department staff on a continual basis throughout the year so that precious organizational time and energy is always focused on what's important. The timing depends on the frequency of data collection, and principals are responsible for communicating data trends to faculty and building support staff.

The superintendent communicates scorecard data trends to the board of education during regularly scheduled meetings and during board workshops. The superintendent takes opportunities to update groups designed to share communications (the Superintendent's Communication Council, the Classroom Teachers Council, The District Advisory Committee on Educational Excellence, and so on) during meetings and to discuss the results the district is producing. District publications and the annual shareholders' report communicate the same information across the district as well as to the community. (See Tables 7.1 and 7.2.)

Here's a quick review of our district-level feedback processes:

- Long-term improvement objectives and targets are aligned to the six key goals.

Table 7.1 District 15's key goals and improvement results.

Key Goals	Improvement Objectives and Measures	2002	2003	2004	2005	2007
21st century skills	Increase student use of quality tools for reasoning and problem-solving by teacher checklist of tools	50%	93%	96%	100%	100%
	Increase number of books read per student per school year	40	49	52	55	60
World-class achievement	Increase % of second graders reading at grade level	84%	84%	96%	100%	100%
	Increase number of subject areas (by grade level) who meet/exceed 90% of state standards (13)	1	NA	8	13	13
	Increase number of student subgroups per subject area who meet/exceed standards (78)	4	NA	18	39	78
	Increase % of student satisfaction with school	81%	78%	85%	90%	100%
	Increase student enthusiasm for learning	68%	87%	90%	90%	95%
Connected learning community	Increase % of parent satisfaction with the quality of education	80%	86%	90%	95%	95%
	Increase % of parent satisfaction with special education programs	91%	93%	94%	95%	95%
	Increase % of parent satisfaction with English language learner	95%	86%	90%	95%	95%
	Increase % of reprographics customer satisfaction	90%	95%	96%	98%	99%
	Increase % satisfied with D15 publications	98%	98%	98%	99%	99%
	Improve relation management by eliminating repeated complaint topics	NA	30	25	20	15
	Increase customer satisfaction with technology department	95%	98%	98%	99%	99%
Caring, safe, and orderly learning environment	Decease % of student accident rate	4%	3%	3%	2%	2%
	Decrease number of student bus conduct notices	1283	855	755	700	685
	Increase % student satisfaction with food services	85%	86%	90%	95%	95%
	Increase % of satisfaction with student-to-student respect	50%	63%	70%	85%	95%
	Decrease number of bus accidents	28	14	12	10	10
High performing staff	Increase % of teacher satisfaction with their school	79%	86%	90%	95%	97%
	Increase support staff satisfaction % with working conditions	92%	94%	96%	98%	99%
	Increase % of new teacher satisfaction with the induction/mentoring programs	88%	100%	100%	100%	100%
	Increase % of minority employees	10.8%	11.4%	14%	23%	32%
	Increase number of National Board Certified Teachers	48	63	80	90	100
	Increase % of satisfaction with new noncertified employee orientation	94%	100%	100%	100%	100%
	Increase support staff training hours	43	47	55	65	75
	Increase number of "best practice" examples posted on Learning Village (District 15 Intranet)	50	100	150	200	250
	Increase % of teachers using whole faculty study group staff development	NA	5%	25%	50%	75%
Aligned and integrated management system	Increase D15 from a band 3 to a band 5 organization	3	NA	5	6	6
	Increase % of bus on-time delivery	98%	99%	99%	99%	99%
	Increase % of network reliability	75%	99.9%	99.9%	99.9%	99.9%
	Decrease technology service cycle time (hours)	25.6	11.4	10	9	8
	Decrease purchase order cycle time (days)	2.1	1.3	1	1	1
	Decrease % of budgeted expenditures	4.05%	4.42%	2.50%	1.50%	1.0%

- Each key goal has success measures (what kind of data are being collected), the type (either leading or in-process data as opposed to lagging or results data), the frequency with which the data are collected, and the collection method.
- Activities of all senior leaders are directed by their One-Page Plan objectives and action plans. Those

Table 7.2 District 15's key goals and success measures.

Key Goals		Success Measures	Type	Frequency	Collection Method
21st century skills		Book circulation	Leading	Monthly	Follett System information
		Book collection	Leading	Monthly	Follett System information
	X	Reasoning tools rubric	Leading	Quarterly	Classroom observation
		Student-to-student respect	Leading	Quarterly	SIP data
		Healthy Fitness Scale	Lagging	Yearly	Fitnessgram
	X	Tech integration rubric	Lagging	Yearly	STAR chart software
		Extracurricular offerings	Leading	Quarterly	Extra duty requests
World-class achievement	X	ISAT Criteria Test (R, M, W, SS, S)	Lagging	Yearly	Students tested in spring
	X	ITBS Standardized Test (R, M, L.A.)	Lagging	Yearly	Students tested in fall
		KIP, FLIP, SAIL tests (R)	Leading	Monthly	Word recognition, comprehension
		SOAR, Read 180 Tests (R)	Leading	Monthly	Reading fluency, comprehension
	X	Logramos ITBS Test (R, M, L.A.)	Lagging	Yearly	Students tested in spring
	X	Assess2Learn Survey Test (M)	Leading	Quarterly	On-line tests
	X	Assess2Learn Diagnostic Tests (R, M, L.A.)	Leading	Daily	On-line tests
		KIP, FLIP, SAIL tests (Spanish) (R)	Leading	Monthly	Word recognition, comprehension
		World-Class Tests (M, P. S.)	Lagging	Every other year	On-line tests from England Curriculum authority
Connected learning community		Parent satisfaction	Lagging	Yearly	Scantron survey
		Parent satisfaction	Leading	Monthly	Telephone survey
		Number of Web-site visits	Leading	Monthly	Web-site software
		Building usage	Leading	Monthly	Building use contracts
		Number of dollars, food, clothing, presentations, and participation in organizations	Lagging	Yearly	Staff and student community participation
		Number of active members	Leading	Monthly	Senior Exchange Report
Caring, safe, and orderly learning environment	X	Student perceptions of safety, caring orderliness	Lagging	Yearly	Student satisfaction survey
	X	Teacher perception of safety and support	Lagging	Yearly	Teacher satisfaction survey
	X	Support staff perceptions of safety and support	Lagging	Yearly	Support staff satisfaction survey
	X	Student focus group perceptions of safety, caring, and orderliness	Leading	Quarterly	Principal facilitated by grade
	X	Teacher focus group perceptions of safety and support	Leading	2/3 per year	External facilitator
	X	Support staff focus group perceptions of safety and support	Leading	2/3 per year	External facilitator
		Number of claimable accidents	Leading	Monthly	Bus accident report
		Number of conduct notices	Leading	Monthly	Bus conduct tracking process
		Bus maintenance	Leading	Daily	Maintenance records
	X	Number of student accidents	Leading	Monthly	Student accident report

Continued

Table 7.2 District 15's key goals and success measures. *Continued*

Key Goals		Success Measures	Type	Frequency	Collection Method
High performing staff	X	Teacher perception of working conditions	Lagging	Yearly	Teacher satisfaction survey
	X	Support staff perceptions of working conditions	Lagging	Yearly	Support staff satisfaction survey
	X	Teacher perceptions of working conditions	Leading	2/3 per year	Teacher focus group
	X	Support staff perceptions of working conditions	Leading	2/3 per year	Support staff focus group
		Number of NBCT certificates issued	Lagging	Yearly	NBCT facilitator
		Number of CPDUs issued	Leading	Monthly	Staff development participation process
		New employee orientation	Leading	Periodically	Orientation survey
		New teacher induction/mentoring	Lagging	Yearly	Participant survey
		Teaching attrition	Lagging	Periodically	Exit interview or survey
	X	Number of teachers recognized	Leading	Periodically	Teacher recognition
		Number absent by employee category	Leading	Daily	Staff absenteeism
Aligned and integrated management system	X	Organizational value-added	Lagging	Yearly	Overall ISAT performance chart
	X	Leadership effectiveness	Lagging	Yearly	Systems check for district leadership teams
	X	Leadership effectiveness	Leading	2/3 per year	Teacher/support staff focus group
		Students exiting special education	Leading	Monthly	Annual review recommendations
		Students exiting second-language	Leading program	Periodically	Second-language Program exit record
	X	Revenues vs. expenditures	Leading	Monthly	Board budget report
	X	Technology effectiveness	Lagging	Yearly	CEO STaR Chart profile
		Network reliability	Leading	Daily	Software tracking "glitches"
		Lunch program effectiveness	Lagging	Yearly	National School Food Service survey
		Bus on-time delivery	Leading	Daily	Asst. Principal check list
	X	Organizational systems effectiveness	Lagging	2 per year	Organizational Effectiveness cycle (OEC)
		Custodial program effectiveness	Leading	2/3 per year	Custodial program survey
		Maintenance program effectiveness	Leading	Monthly	Work order issued vs. completed end time
	X	Aggregated school complaints by category	Leading	Quarterly	Complaint tracking process

objectives and action plans are directly aligned to the district key goals. Monthly or quarterly feedback mechanisms are built into each One-Page Plan for both objectives and action plan progress, which is one of the reasons we chose this management methodology. NOTE: This alignment of senior leader activity to the district mission would not be possible if the board of education had not established the accomplishment of the key goals (see Chapter 3) in the strategic plan as a five-year process.

Education Data Warehouse (EDW)

The ultimate question that everyone in our organizations needs to answer is, "What works, for which students, over time?" If you are a service provider, the question is, "What works, for which customers, over time?" In order to answer that question, you must have organized data. We didn't have organized data. We had unorganized data, missing data, and data that, frankly, were unintentionally (or in some cases, maybe intentionally) hidden.

Data have to be organized around the questions you want the data to answer. IBM was contracted to lead us through a discovery process to determine what questions we wanted the EDW to answer. District and IBM staff teamed together over many focus group meetings and survey results analysis to discover and validate the primary EDW requirements for our district. During this discovery process, 19 questions were identified as being most likely to help us answer the "What works?" question. The answers to these questions became the data design and acquisition focus of the EDW and guided development and deployment throughout the implementation of our Phase I EDW. The questions were:

1. What are our national standardized and state criterion referenced results and trends?
2. What are the quartile and cut score distributions for our national standardized and state criterion referenced tests?
3. What are the characteristics of students making the most dramatic test score gains/losses?
4. What are student growth trends by subjects?
5. What are the growth trends for a grade level/school by subjects?
6. What is the student's enrollment history?
7. What are the attendance patterns and trends?
8. How do students who have been in attendance in the district for varying amounts of time perform on tests?
9. How have enrollment demographics in the school/cluster changed?
10. What are the significant trends in discipline issues?

11. What is the relationship between retention and intervention?
12. What programs are effective?
13. Does summer school improve student achievement?
14. How are students in special programs performing on tests?
15. Which special education students are progressing year to year?
16. How many students are fluent speakers of languages other than English and what are trends in this area?
17. How well do second language students achieve after exiting the English Language Learner (ELL) program?
18. What is the current status of gap analyses across schools and clusters by subject, ethnicity, gender, and socioeconomic status?
19. What are the patterns of reported student satisfaction and enthusiasm for learning across grade level, school, cluster, and district?

After scouring the district to find the data, the information had to be cleansed (free of errors) and loaded into the warehouse. More than 200 preformatted reports were developed to answer the 19 questions. Approximately 300 variables can be combined and/or disaggregated (socioeconomic status, grade level, subject, attendance, nationality, program, school, cohorts, and so on) to build these preformatted reports.

To give you an idea of the types of data found in the EDW, the top five most-requested reports are:

1. Reports on which students are overachievers, achieving at expected levels, and underachievers
2. Reports about which students and which groups of students are not meeting state standards
3. Performance trends related to subgroups of students (minority, language, IEPs, socioeconomic status, and so on)
4. Reports on which students are "bubble students" (bubble students are those students who are "on the

bubble" or right on the cut score between meeting/not meeting state standards)

5. Continuous enrollment reports (cohort trends)

Other types of reports show the relationship between student attendance and achievement. In the 2001-2002 school year, the difference between missing 0-8 days and 17 or more days of school is 19 points on the state Illinois Standards Achievement Test (ISAT) assessment. In our district, that is the difference between getting a B or a D. Not insignificant. Even more importantly, consider how useful this information would be in the hands of a building administrator or teacher when talking to a parent about attendance problems.

A scattergram can be used to show the performance relationship for different kinds of tests over a two-year period. This report answers the question, "Is school performance growing, staying the same, or declining?" It also gives the building principal and district senior leaders a very important piece of information about the difference between the lowest and highest performing schools. We know that a community will stand only so much difference in performance between schools before they start to ask uncomfortable questions like, "Why does performance differ so much between these schools?" This report helps us track that gap so we can continually work on closing the variance and increasing the mean.

That's the "hard" side of the EDW. It also has a "soft" side. There we include data from our student and teacher surveys.

- Teacher surveys include Conditions of Teaching (a teacher satisfaction survey) and shared decision making (a survey designed to assess how well shared decision making is being practiced in the school).
- Student surveys, printed in both English and Spanish, include a satisfaction (Grades 3-8) and a student enthusiasm for learning (Grades K-8) survey. We survey ninth-grade students about their junior high experience in October or November, after they have adjusted to high school and can critique those things that are helping and hindering their success. The ninth-grade feedback process also includes a focus group to validate the survey data.

- School support staff and department staff satisfaction surveys help us to better understand work-related issues and identify satisfiers and dissatisfiers.
- Parent surveys are segmented by regular program parents, special education, and second-language parents.

To give you an example of the numbers, the average level of teacher satisfaction over the past five years has risen from 67 percent to 86 percent. If you look closer at the numbers, seven percent of the teachers are actually dissatisfied and seven percent are not sure or neither satisfied or dissatisfied (see Figure 7.1). In 2000-2001, the variance between school staff when answering the question, "My school is a safe and secure place to work and learn" ranged from a high of 100 to a low of 17 percent. The following year, asking the same question, the high was again 100 but the low was 91 percent. For every question on the survey, the low score has moved up and the district average has increased.

A very strict rule-of-thumb we enforce is that we never use one point of data for analysis. We always talk about trends, and we much prefer run or control charts to display and discuss what the data mean.

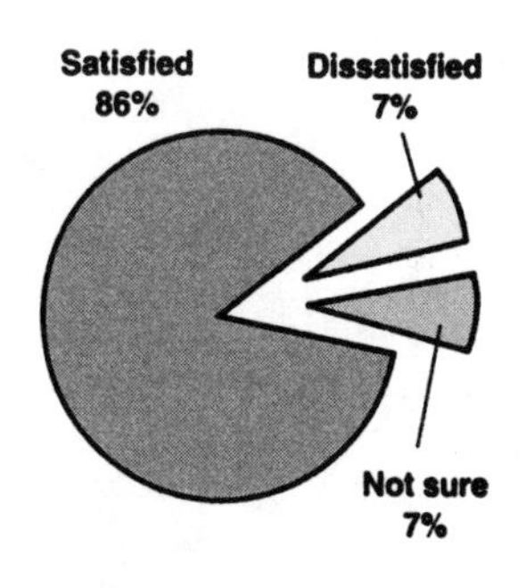

Figure 7.1 Teacher satisfaction.

Internal Assessment

We use the Baldrige framework to audit both educational and support operations in our district. These audit questions are used in a specific sequence during department visits or in talks with department leaders.

Audit Questions

1. Who are your department/school/classroom customers and what do they want? How do you know what they want?
2. What are the short-term (this year) and long-term (two to three years) goals for your department/school/classroom?
3. How do you define leadership in your department/school/classroom?

4. Do you have the right information at the right time to make effective decisions?

5. Is your department/school/classroom staff/student-body skilled and motivated to achieve what customers want? How do you know if they are skilled and motivated?

6. Are your department/school/classroom processes efficient and effective? What data do you analyze to know if processes are efficient and effective?

7. Is your department/school/classroom meeting or exceeding customer expectations? How do you know?

As Mark Blazey has so clearly pointed out in his graphic version of the Baldrige categories, the framework is built on the foundation of the Information and Analysis Category.[7] If everyone, and we mean everyone, does not have the right information and the right time to make effective decisions, the rest of the framework cannot function properly. We can't go overboard and blame people in the organization for not getting the results we want if they don't have the information they need to analyze and make informed decisions. This is a systems breakdown and needs to be fixed immediately. Our experience strongly suggests that if you have to make a decision about what to fix first, work on this category right after you finish creating a strategic plan with measurable goals or targets.

Semiannually, the leadership team (central office senior leaders and building principals) meets for a day-long organizational performance review. The team analyzes the full range of data available to see if mid-course and end-of-year corrections are needed. We modeled this from a business approach developed by the Franklin Covey Company called the Organizational Effectiveness Cycle. We have enhanced the model by overlaying the Baldrige criteria at the appropriate steps to further refine the self-assessment approach within the cycle. Our enhanced model is referred to as Charting the Course (see Figure 7.2).

The analysis of district performance begins with a *diagnosis phase* where gaps between current performance and desired goals and targets are identified and root causes for those gaps are determined. A *design phas*e aligns the organization's systems so that areas of high performance are

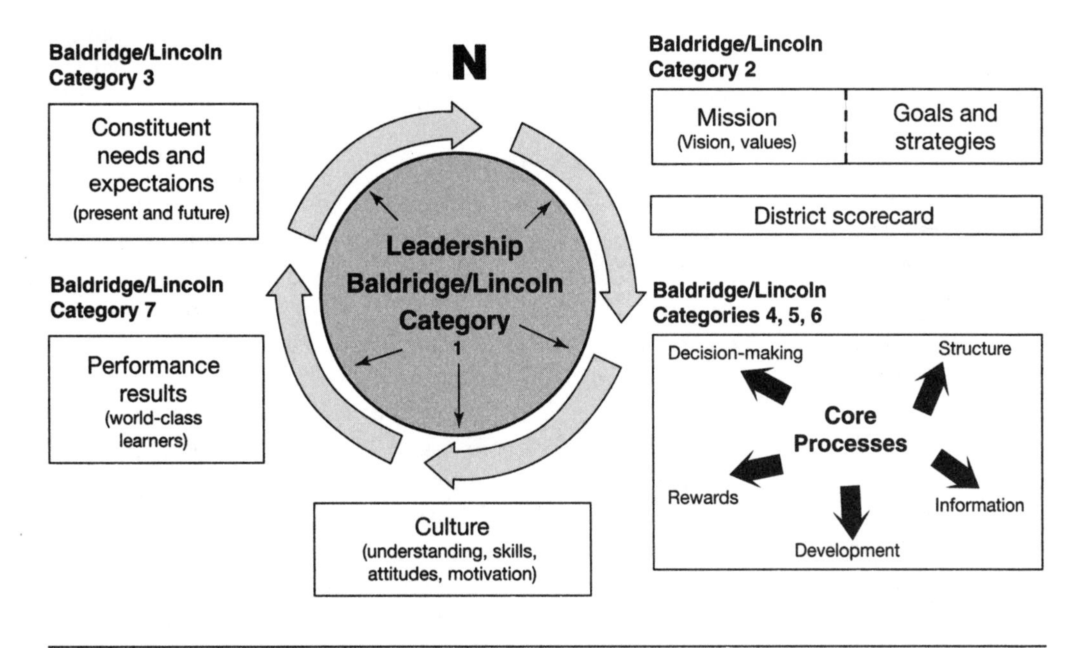

Figure 7.2 Charting the course.
Adapted from Steven R. Covey, *Principle-Centered Leadership.*

maintained while improvements are developed to close gaps. The *deliver phase* focuses on deploying the newly refined systems and monitoring system performance through the collection of process data and frequent analysis of those data. The diagnosis phase rotates through the Charting the Course framework in a counterclockwise motion. The design and deliver phases move clockwise.

The *diagnosis phase* is set in the context of achieving the district mission by accomplishing the key goals and student performance targets. It begins with reviewing customer and other stakeholder needs and expectations. Balanced scorecard data are used to determine where results are meeting established targets and where gaps exist. The district culture is analyzed to determine gaps in performance and what knowledge, skills, attitudes, and/or levels of motivation are causing those gaps. Because the culture is determined by the systems in which people work, data from the core processes are used to assess effectiveness and determine what improvements should by made. Based on this analysis, the *design* phase identifies the "vital" few priorities that can leverage significant improvements in organizational performance, and describes how strategy and core processes will change to affect the culture and improve results. The *deliver* phase uses the PDSA continuous improvement cycle to try out the improvement theory, study the results, and either standardize improvements or improve the design.

Comparative Data

THE USE OF COMPARATIVE DATA IS LIKE SCANNING YOUR WIND DIRECTION IN A SAILBOAT. YOU NEED TO KNOW THE DIRECTION IN ORDER TO TRIM YOUR SAILS PROPERLY (OR IN QUALITY TERMS, ALIGN THEM) SO YOUR VESSEL WILL MOVE SMOOTHLY AHEAD IN THE RIGHT DIRECTION. WE LIKEN SUCH DATA TO THE "TELLTALES" ON A SHIP'S SAIL. THESE SMALL LENGTHS OF YARD (GREEN FOR STARBOARD AND RED FOR PORT) ATTACHED TO THE SAIL GIVE SAILORS A VISUAL REFERENCE FOR DETERMINING WHICH WAY THE WIND IS BLOWING ... SO ON YOUR JOURNEY, IT'S A GOOD IDEA TO CHECK YOUR TELLTALES FREQUENTLY.

Any judgment about how well an organization is performing requires comparative data. Baldrige would say that any concept of performance excellence requires comparisons with comparable organizations and appropriate best-in-class benchmarks. We use comparative data to show how our performance compares with other organizations similar to ours and to ones that we call benchmarks. Similar organization data gives a good perspective on performance, but benchmark comparisons give you a perspective related to the best. Both are useful when judging the performance of your organization.

The use of comparative data creates a constant challenge to ensure apples-to-apples comparisons. Demographic, economic, geographic, and financial variables make decisions about comparability difficult, but not impossible. One problem we confront is that we collect data (for example, student enthusiasm for learning) that other school districts don't collect. This requires constant scanning of various national, state, and local sources to find comparative data. It also requires branching out into the private sector to find similar services and measures. Department leaders/managers are required to seek out appropriate comparative organizations or services and request their data. Persistence is sometimes necessary, as the practice of exchanging comparative data is not necessarily a common practice. Department leaders/managers analyze the comparative data they obtain to see how well they perform, to identify best practices, and to use benchmarking to see if adoption or adaptation will help improve their department services and processes.

ENDNOTES

1. Blake, William. 1790. *The marriage of heaven and hell.*
2. Collins, Jim. 2001. *Good to great: Why some companies make the leap and others don't.* New York: Harper Collins.
3. Harry, Mikel J. and Richard Schroeder. 1999. *Six sigma: The breakthrough management strategy revolutionizing the world's top corporations.* New York: Doubleday.

4. Walberg, Herbert J. 2002. *School accountability: An assessment by the Koret Task Force on K-12 education.* Stanford, CA: Hoover Institution.
5. Elmore, Richard. 2002. The price of accountability, *Results* (November).
6. Heiss, Frederick. 2003. Resist urge to refine graduation testing. *The Gladfly: Education news and analysis from the Thomas B. Fordham Foundation.*
7. Blazey, Mark, Karen Davison, and John Evans. 2003. *Insights to performance excellence in education*, Milwaukee: ASQ Quality Press.

8

Reading Your Compass: Aligning Organizational Culture to Performance Improvement

If organizational improvement is to be truly effective, all facets of the organization must be aligned in the same direction. We had always allowed our schools a significant degree of autonomy—but now, we were asking them to use their compasses to navigate on the same course as the district.

If the balanced scorecard is the district business plan, then the SIP is the school's business plan. This chapter will explore the key components of an effective school improvement planning process and describe, in detail, what is required to make the process work.

We believe SIPs are critically important because we know that effective schools do make a difference in student achievement. We can finally lay to rest the notion that everything except the school determines the performance levels of students. Yes, the teacher effect is larger (Marzano), but when effective teachers are found in effective schools, the results are impressive, even amazing.[1]

To understand the power of a standardized SIP, you only have to look at the historical issues that accompany this process. District 15 has been using the SIP process for many years, but our results had been mixed, at best. There was broad district-level and state support for school level improvement, and our school staffs were spending significant amounts of time creating and implementing their best efforts at SIPs, but what we were doing clearly wasn't working! SIP issues that were impeding this process included school goals that were not aligned to district goals and expectations, goals that focused on implementing new programs

PRIOR TO THE DEVELOPMENT OF THE MAGNETIC COMPASS, SEAFARERS USED BOTH PRIMITIVE INSTRUMENTS (THE ANCIENT WIND ROSE) AND NATURAL PHENOMENA (WAVE SIZE AND DIRECTION OR STARS) TO RECKON THEIR COURSES. ACCORDING TO THE *ANNAPOLIS BOOK OF SEAMANSHIP*, "NO ONE KNOWS WHEN EXACTLY, BUT SOMETIME BEFORE THE 11TH CENTURY A.D., SEAMEN BEGAN TO MEASURE THEIR PROGRESS AGAINST ANOTHER, BUT MUCH LESS TANGIBLE, CONSTANT—THE EARTH'S MAGNETIC FIELD ... A PRIMITIVE COMPASS WAS A STICK FLOATING IN A BOWL OF WATER AND SUPPORTING A PIECE OF MAGNETIZED MATERIAL POINTING AT MAGNETIC NORTH."

THE BALDRIGE CRITERIA BECAME OUR TRUE NORTH—A CONSTANT AGAINST WHICH WE COULD MEASURE OUR PROGRESS.

and processes (the classical confusion between means and ends) rather than on achieving results. (See the Outcome Statements on p. 99 for examples of results goals.) Each year new goals would be developed, even if the previous goals had not been achieved. Accountability was focused on developing SIPs each year, not on achieving results. SIPs were almost completely devoid of leading or in-process measures, and in some cases, of any measures at all.

The lack of a powerful results-oriented SIP process became a critical problem because when we took a close look at student performance trends, some patterns became clear:

- The lagging indicators (our state and national standardized tests) were not improving significantly, and some had even declined slightly.
- Subgroup performance was not acceptable.
- Student behavior and attitudes toward learning and subjects was not measured.
- 21st century skills were being almost universally neglected.

These results were obviously not acceptable, and the school leadership agreed. Principals and building staff were frustrated at playing the SIP game without being able to show results for their hard work. The process was a waste of their time. We all knew it, but we had a hard time saying it. Reflecting our belief that this was not a people (or building leadership) problem, we recognized that the problem was the system—or as it often turns out, the lack of a system.

We had trained leadership teams of administrators and teachers in each school in the principles and practices of continuous improvement and the school improvement process. Like many school districts, we had an understanding—although some would say a superficial grasp—of the PDSA improvement cycle. Other organizations successfully use the principles and practices of continuous improvement, most often in the form of PDSA, so our approach clearly wasn't the problem.

The question was, what was the "right" system to put in place? One obvious issue was that our SIPs were not necessarily aligned to district goals and the student performance targets. The lack of accountability was also an issue.

It was apparent that we needed to create a more clearly articulated SIP process that would increase the school staff's ownership of the process and ease their struggle over what an SIP should be and do. We also had a laundry list of other attributes our ideal SIP process should incorporate: It would have to be compatible with our beliefs about how organizations learn and improve. It would have to be comprehensive but easy to learn and use. It would have to be tied to the evaluation of the building principal. It would have to be based on systems thinking. In addition, we knew that the revised process needed to be easily available, accountability had to be apparent, and knowledge and skill sharing across the organization had to be a part of the process. (See Figure 8.1.)

We began to revise our SIP process by thinking about the system into which SIP must fit, and we looked to the systems experts for guidance. Deming created a flowchart to demonstrate the components of a system that produces something of value.[2] Lee Jenkins offered a wonderful variation of Deming's flowchart to describe education as a system.[3] We began to fill in the specifics of the Jenkins flowchart to describe the major

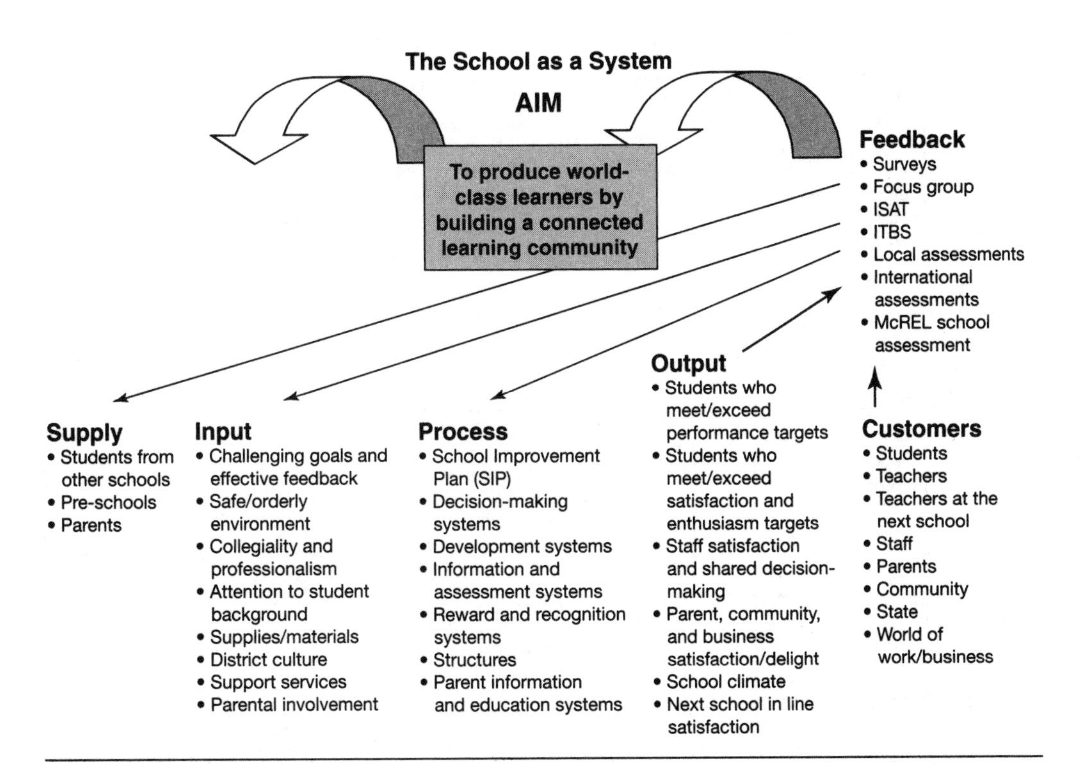

Figure 8.1 System alignment.

variables that influence the education system from our perspective, including where SIP fit into that system.

Completing this flowchart prepared us for designing a new SIP process. It enabled us to more clearly understand how customer wants and expectations and the school's current output (analyzed from various forms of feedback and filtered through the district's mission) fit and influenced SIP. Specifically defining supply, input, and process issues also helped with the design process, because these are the major variables that either support or should be incorporated into a SIP process (see Figure 8.2).

We decided to embed the revised process electronically in our Learning Village Intranet, although a paper and pencil format would have been a good second choice. We found two valuable resources by benchmarking other SIP processes throughout the nation. One was a flowchart from a North Carolina school district that sparked our thinking about the steps in the SIP process. The second was a month-by-month timeline that we modified from the Maryland State

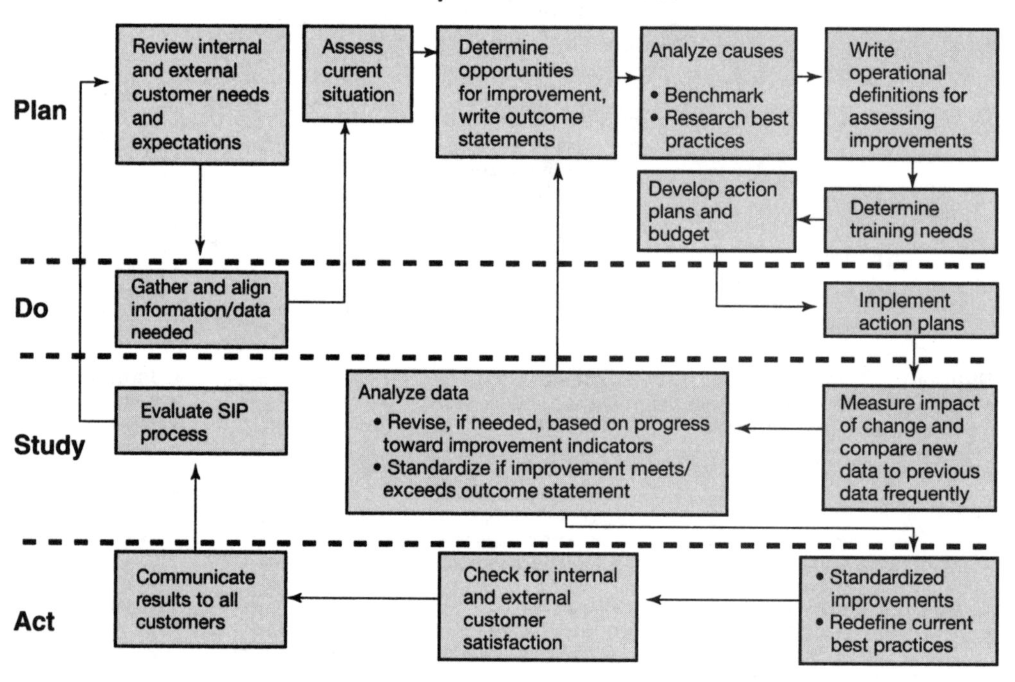

Figure 8.2 Improvement plan model.

Department of Education example that shows the progression of SIP activities during the course of the year.

Our redesign standardized the SIP process so that the focus is on the student performance targets (see p. 75). These specific, measurable goals reflect the district's definition of world-class learning, and although they are definitely challenging, we are convinced that they are attainable by 2005. In fact, several schools have already achieved many of these board-determined goals. When the first school achieved all of the specific measurable goals, the superintendent made a surprise visit to a morning faculty meeting to bring his congratulations—and dozens of delicious, fresh doughnuts as a small tangible reward.

The standardized SIP process begins by consulting the SIP calendar (see Table 8.1). The calendar, used by the SIP steering committee to guide the improvement process throughout the year, describes the month-by-month steps in the process, the involvement required from the staff and SIP steering committee, and activities between staff and SIP steering committee meetings.

SIP steering committee membership usually comprises staff members who are on goal teams. Schools ask staff members to be SIP participants by being on a goal team that has the responsibility for carrying out the action plan steps, collecting and analyzing leading or in-process data, and reporting progress back to the building staff on a regular basis. Representatives from these goal teams coordinate schoolwide improvement efforts through the SIP steering committee.

The next step is to go to the "School Improvement That Works" site on our Intranet. School administrators requested the development of an electronic site that had all the steps, information, data, tools, and forms available for the planning process at the click of a mouse button. This electronic site has helped make the planning process much more efficient and effective. The steering committee or our entire staff (depending on the activity) can quickly and easily access a description of the process and related data and documents by clicking on any of the shaded boxes or steps in the process.

Before setting goals for a new school year, staff members review last year's SIP, analyze the gaps between where they are currently and want to be in the future, determine the root cause of these gaps, develop outcome statements, discuss theories of improvement, and develop a plan of action. This is the *Plan* phase of the SIP process.

Table 8.1 District 15 school improvement plan calendar.

June, July and August	Staff Meeting	SIP Steering Committee Meeting	Activities Between Meetings
Begin plan for next school year:			
Review internal and external customer needs and expectations (Plan)	Review internal customer needs/expectations trend data: • Staff surveys		Review SIP at June LTM
Gather and align information/data (Plan)	• Student surveys • Student Performance target data	Access the EDW to analyze trend data and identify and disaggregate student performance.	
Assess current situation (Plan)	• Mission data • Internal review		
Determine opportunities for improvement (Plan)	Review external customer needs/expectations trend data:	Make recommendations for SIP goals	
Analyze causes (Plan)	• Parent satisfaction • Community satisfaction		
Write operational definitions (Plan)	Analyze current data in the EDW		Write operational definitions for assessing improvements
Determine training needs (Plan)	Determine SIP goals for next school year	Prioritize training needs	
Conduct an internal review self-assessment (Plan)	Discuss training needs assessment data		Complete training needs assessment
	Conduct an internal review self-assessment using Shipley Systems Check – Level II (classroom, school support staff, or program specialist)	Aggregate and analyze results from the internal self-assessment summary report and send an electronic copy to department of instruction	Principal/SIP steering committee chair arrange for training or information needs Schedule training activities

The *Do* phase of the SIP process tests improvement theories. The outcome is to collect in-process data for analysis by the staff. When they identify an improvement theory or theories in the *Plan* phase, they use their understanding of best practices and benchmarked programs to make decisions about what improvements to implement. But until they implement the improvement theory and collect data about its effectiveness, they still don't know how effective these improvements will be in reducing the performance gap. Carrying out the improvement theory according to the plan is always a complicated issue with time and schedules ranking right at the top of the list. This usually requires some training of those involved, including methods of collecting data and the importance of closely following the improvement plan. Staff activities during this time include reviewing the SIP calendar and planning suggested activities. Because examples are many times the best teachers of teachers, staff members find opportunities to showcase stories of how teachers are collecting and using data to improve instruction during staff meetings and other school activities. Around November, the end of the first quarter of the school year, the staff review the progress made toward accomplishing our school improvement goals.

December is always a good time for celebrations, and during the first quarter of the school year, the staff takes time to celebrate successes. The results of the Iowa Test of Basic Skills (ITBS) arrive at the end of November and are loaded into our electronic data warehouse so data can be analyzed to see if revisions or adjustments of SIP goals are necessary. Any benchmarking activities should be completed and shared with staff to gain new insights about promising practices.

During the *Study* phase of the SIP process, the staff reviews the data they are collecting to see if the improvement theory is actually working. The outcome of this phase is to take the in-process data collected in the *Do* phase and make data-based decisions to determine whether the changes made are resulting in genuine improvement. Without this step in the process, the staff may be making changes that aren't bringing improvements or possibly making improvements that don't meet the needs of all students. Staff members pay close attention to the impact of the improvements and compare new data to previous data frequently to identify trends.

During January, February, and March, the staff continues to implement action plans, measuring the impact of change and studying performance trends. At staff meetings, you would see data analysis tools being used (run charts, Pareto diagrams, radar charts, bar charts, and histograms to draw pictures of the data) to better interpret the results and make decisions about needed enhancements to the improvement theory. Although no one wants this to occur, the *Study* step

RECKONING—TO CALCULATE A SHIP'S POSITION BY PLOTTING ON THE CHART THE DISTANCE RUN SINCE THE LAST RELIABLE NAVIGATIONAL FIX, TAKING INTO ACCOUNT SPEED, TIDE, CURRENT, WIND, AND ANY OTHER FACTORS THAT MIGHT HAVE INFLUENCED FORWARD MOTION THROUGH THE WATER. IN MODERN TIMES, THE TERM HAS BOTH ITS NAUTICAL NAVIGATIONAL MEANING AND A SIMILAR CONSTRUCTION APPLIED TO AN ACTIVITY INVOLVING SEQUENTIAL STEPS OF SOME KIND, WHEREIN AN ESTIMATE OF ONE'S PROGRESS OR PERFORMANCE MUST BE MADE FROM TIME TO TIME.

–AN OCEAN OF WORDS, P. 134

sometimes bring discouraging news that the improvement theory isn't creating the improvements wanted. Then staff members cycle back to the *Plan* phase and start over again, exactly as the flowchart directs them. If they do a good job of planning, this shouldn't happen. If our results verify that our improvement is achieving results, we are ready to move on to the "standardize improvements" step.

The staff closes the loop of the SIP process during the *Act* phase by making decisions based on studying trend data during the school year. If they are satisfied, even delighted, with the performance of students, and know they will meet or exceed the goal, then it's time to standardize the process. Standardizing the process means that all the changes made, are reviewed, documented, and implemented to minimize the chances of reverting to the pre-improvement state. This also means that they might have to plan for some follow-up training or coaching and monitor future changes very carefully.

The staff is usually involved in the *Act* phase of the SIP process during the months of April and May. The first, second, and third quarters of the school year will have given enough time to implement the improvement theory and collect enough data about its effectiveness so that the staff can make the decision to standardize or revise. They want to make sure there are convincing trends in the data collected to be confident that the improvement theory works well. In many cases, they will be pleased with some of the improvements made but will want to continue to improve other parts of the theory. If this is the case, they begin planning those improvements during May. The SIP steering committee spends time planning for recognizing and celebrating the improvements in student performance during the year, but May is the time for real celebrations. It is a great staff achievement to take on an improvement goal and use the SIP process to achieve better results.

With careful planning and gathering of relevant data, the staff has valid evidence to confirm the improvement theory or to modify it. The end result of a SIP ought to be that it shows a clear plan and description about how the school is helping the district accomplish its mission.

What made the real difference in our revised SIP process? Several things:

1. First was the shift to a focus on student performance targets—and only these targets. *No other goals are permissible.* Before, as we

described earlier, SIP goals often focused on implementing something (for example, a reading program improvement, a discipline plan, a teaming approach, or cooperative learning). The assumption was that if the program or practice improvements were implemented, student performance would improve. While this may seem a reasonable assumption, district test scores usually firmly refuted the assumption. Our SIP process now reflects the understanding that implementing such programs may be important—but only if the result is improved student performance.

2. The second is that we flowcharted the SIP process and attached specific activities that had to be accomplished during each step in the flowchart. This clarified 99 percent of the confusion about what was to be done at any given step in the process. After all, if you can't illustrate the various steps of a process with a flowchart, you can't determine where to improve it.

3. The third revision that made a difference was having the sources of data and information available electronically to school decision makers as they did their gap analysis. Actionable data are now delivered to building staff instantly so that time can be spent analyzing and making judgments about the data, not in seeking out the data. Seven years of demographic data are reviewed to determine whether trends are shifting relative to income, second language enrollment, mobility, and minority status. Those trends are compared to district and state data. (Demographic data should be used to help analyze data and understand the complexities of school improvement. These data should never be used as an excuse or a rationalization against improvement.) Included in the data are School Projection Reports (see Figure 8.3) displaying data in all subject/grade level areas beginning in the year 2000 and projecting gains or losses by year to see if current trends in achievement will accomplish the student performance targets by the goal date of 2005.

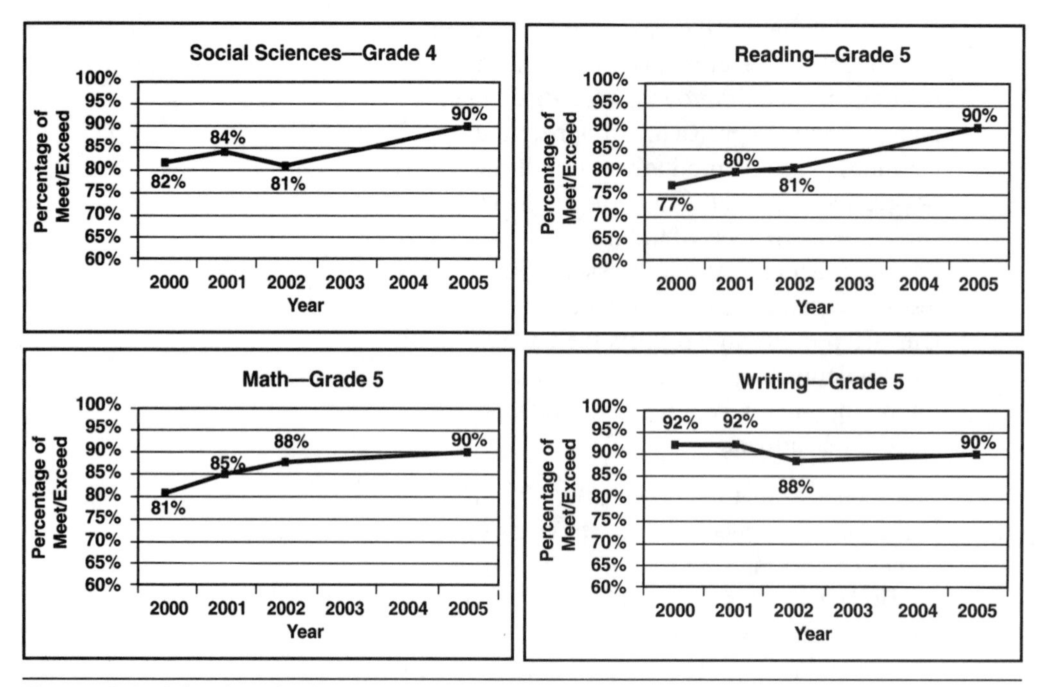

Figure 8.3 School projections.

4. The fourth improvement helped to standardize improvement strategies. We programmed into the SIP site all district-developed and approved instructional improvement strategies so that building staff could, if they wished, choose from this list as they developed their improvement theories. Our schools have freedom to choose any researched "best" practice they think will improve student performance, but having the strategies listed and available made decisions easier. Most school staff now choose strategies from the district-approved list.

5. The fifth major revision to the SIP process was the development of an "Outcome Statement for Improvement." This is a fairly standard practice in many organizations, but it wasn't in place in our district. Outcomes state the end results that the school staff wants to achieve. To help develop that outcome statement, they answer the following questions:

   - What will change?
   - Among whom?

- How much change do you expect?
- How will the change be measured?
- By when do you expect to achieve this change?

Outcome statements might look like the following:

- By April 2003, reading scores will improve among the students in fifth grade to 84 percent, meeting or exceeding state standards as measured using the spring Illinois Standards Achievement Test reading assessment.

- By May 2003, reading will improve among the students in second grade who entered District 15 in kindergarten to 100 percent reading at or above grade level as measured using the February Iowa Test of Basic Skills reading total and/or in May using an Individualized Reading Inventory score at the instructional level.

- By May 2003, reading comprehension will improve for all students receiving KIP, FLIP, SAIL, and Si Puedo, (district-developed reading intervention programs in kindergarten, first-, and second-grade, and in the second language program) to 100 percent at or above grade level as measured by their running records and an Individualized Reading Inventory score at the instructional level.

- By May 2003, reading enthusiasm will improve to 80 percent of all students rating it as a 4 or 5 on the enthusiasm scale on the spring District Student Enthusiasm Survey.

6. The last revision that significantly changed the SIP process was the requirement for the construction of a SIP storyboard. The storyboard is a display of the data, analysis, and decisions made during the four PDSA phases of the SIP process. It utilizes graphs, charts, diagrams, matrices, and other display methods to tell the "story" of each SIP goal with a minimal use of text. As building staff work through the steps of the flowchart, they create visuals and

graphs so that information about the SIP is current and readily available. The storyboard is posted in a visible location to allow school staff, parents, and community visitors to quickly scan the display and understand the current status of the SIP. Some schools create a wall or bulletin board display in an area of the building that is accessible to students, staff, parents, and community members. Others create a plan on an 11" x 17" page that can be displayed and disseminated frequently.

Before we made these process changes, we had concluded that we either needed to approach SIP as though it made a difference—or abandon the process entirely. We believe our redesign clearly has made a positive difference. If our principals and building staffs were to describe the redesigned SIP process, they would likely say something like this:

> *"The SIP provides a specific plan for us to use to accomplish the student performance targets and produce world-class learners, and it provides the board of education and our community with the oversight it needs to be assured that improvement is happening."*

As Stephen Robbins pointed out, setting specific, high expectations helps to create a higher level of staff performance and satisfaction with work, and our experience has borne this out.[4]

The new SIP process makes continuous improvement a part of each building's culture because it's practiced daily. It achieves results, and we have the data to prove it!

ENDNOTES

1. Marzano, Robert J. 2003. *What works in schools: Translating research into action*. Alexandria, VA: ASCD.
2. Deming, W. Edwards. 2000. *The new economics for industry, government, education*, 2nd ed. Cambridge, MA: The MIT Press.
3. Jenkins, Lee. 2003. *Improving student learning*, 2nd edition. Milwaukee: ASQ Quality Press.
4. Robbins, Stephen P. 2002. *The truth about managing people ... and nothing but the truth*. Englewood Cliffs, NJ: Prentice Hall.

9

Anchoring: The Holding Power of Continuous Improvement in the Classroom

In our district, one of the first things that occurs each new school year is a "Back-to-School" day where parents meet their child's teacher and see the classroom. Each teacher is charged with communicating his or her expectations for students and parents, as well as for determining parents' expectations. Sometime during the orientation, the teacher asks parents to answer three questions (usually, these are given to parents in written form with blank spaces for their answers):

1. What do you expect you child to learn this year in my class?
2. What do you expect of me in my role as your child's teacher?
3. What do you expect of yourselves as parents?

WHETHER YOU'RE "DROPPING THE HOOK" FOR A BRIEF LUNCH STOP IN A QUIET COVE OR FOR SEVERAL MONTHS IN A TROPICAL PORT, ANCHORING IS PERHAPS THE QUINTESSENTIAL SEAMAN'S ACT, FOR IT COMBINES CAREFUL PLANNING, SENSITIVITY TO WEATHER AND CURRENT, KNOWLEDGE OF YOUR EQUIPMENT, AND CONTINUOUS WATCHFULNESS.

—*THE ANNAPOLIS BOOK OF SEAMANSHIP*, P. 300

The answers to these questions can be unexpected—and sometimes, even unrealistic. One kindergarten parent told the teacher that her role should be "to build future heroes to save the planet Earth." Of course, we know parents want their sons and daughters to be able to reach their potential, grow, and progress; expand thinking and understanding; gather and organize information; develop reasoning, problem solving, and critical thinking skills; and grow to become responsible adults and citizens. We have always known that parents—in fact, the entire community—have high expectations for teachers, but creating heroes is probably a bit beyond what most teachers can achieve in a year. But then again, maybe not.

We do know that good teaching matters a lot to a student's current and future life. For instance, if you classify teachers as "highly effective," "moderately effective," or "ineffective" as measured by student achievement, you will see results like this:

- Students of ineffective teachers demonstrated poor levels of achievement across the board, regardless of the students' prior level of achievement.[1]
- When placed in classrooms with increased teacher effectiveness, students with lower prior achievement were the first to benefit, but only teachers of the highest effectiveness were generally effective with all students.[2]
- A student who is taught by highly effective teachers for three consecutive years will have a cumulative percentile point gain of 83. A student who has teachers who are ineffective for that same three-year period has a cumulative percentile point gain of 29.[3]

It's easy, looking at the research just reviewed, to reach this conclusion: if highly effective teachers taught all students, there would be no achievement gap.

Most of us in education are aware of an insidious rationalization that tries to refute the irrefutable research about teacher effectiveness: the student background argument. This rationalization uses the number of parents a student has, the parents' level of education, their socioeconomic level, the student's nationality and primary language, the student's race, the student's level of motivation, vocabulary, and other extraneous background variables as the reason why certain students can't learn and why there is an achievement gap.

Haycock, Jerald, and Huang say it best: "The American education system has been in thrall to a myth for more than 30 years. The myth says that student achievement has much more to do with a child's background than with the quality of instruction he or she receives … The myth is powerful. It is pervasive. And it is wrong."[4] Many others have powerful and clear research or syntheses of research that refute this false, but hard-to-slay, myth.

Despite all this evidence, some administrators and teachers still believe the myth, or at least proceed with business as usual as if they do. We think these individuals ought to be asked the question: "If you don't believe all students can be learn and be academically successful, which specific students do you believe will not succeed, and how do you plan to share this information with their parents?" When teacher applicants are being interviewed, we think they should be asked: "How many students in your classroom do you believe can meet or exceed our academic standards?" If the answer is anything less than "all of them," those individuals should not be hired. It is not student demographics that make a difference in student achievement, it is the quality and teaching ability of the teacher. But although there is convincing research that identifies the teacher as the educator who most impacts student achievement, that does not absolve senior leaders of responsibility for student achievement gaps.

If it is the quality of the teacher and teaching ability that matters, then how do we, as educational leaders, assure teacher quality? As we described in Chapter 4, the reason higher levels of quality aren't reached and gaps in achievement still exist between groups of students is because district systems aren't aligned. They simply aren't designed correctly to attain their intended purpose. The quality and ability of the teachers is determined by the systems the organization has designed and deployed to motivate and enable faculty and staff to, as the Baldrige criteria say, develop and utilize their full potential.

It is the senior leaders' responsibility to design and deploy systems that place highly effective teachers in highly effective school systems. How might a senior leader approach this task?

The Classroom as a System

The first thing a senior leader should ask about the classroom system is: What classroom processes do we measure and what do the data say about how effective they are? The measures found in Chapter 7 give some good examples of data that can help senior leaders understand how well the district and classroom systems are functioning. Minority hiring, the number of National Board Certified Teachers, the teacher absence reporting system, the quality of substitutes, the history of contract negotiations, the effectiveness of the induction/mentoring program, and training and staff development results are examples of system measures and are ones we use in our district, although they obviously do not measure classroom systems directly.

A radical concept to think about is to view the classroom itself as a system (see Figure 9.1). It is a revelation to many teachers, and to a lot of administrators, to hear the classroom defined as a system. The classroom has outputs, customers, feedback, and exists within a school and district system with common aims. It also has suppliers, inputs, and processes. The components under each system category may vary from district to district, but the categories of the system will be the same.

What the teacher does to understand and improve this system causes student achievement to soar. For example, the teachers in our schools pay a great deal of attention to the supplier-customer chain. They don't describe it that way, but that's what it is. Given this emphasis, who do teachers consider to be their customers? At least one answer might be: the teachers at the next grade level, subject area, or school. Teachers understand that they need to seek out feedback and have discussions about what satisfies these customers as well as how satisfied they are with the students they receive. They are expected to spend time with their customers to

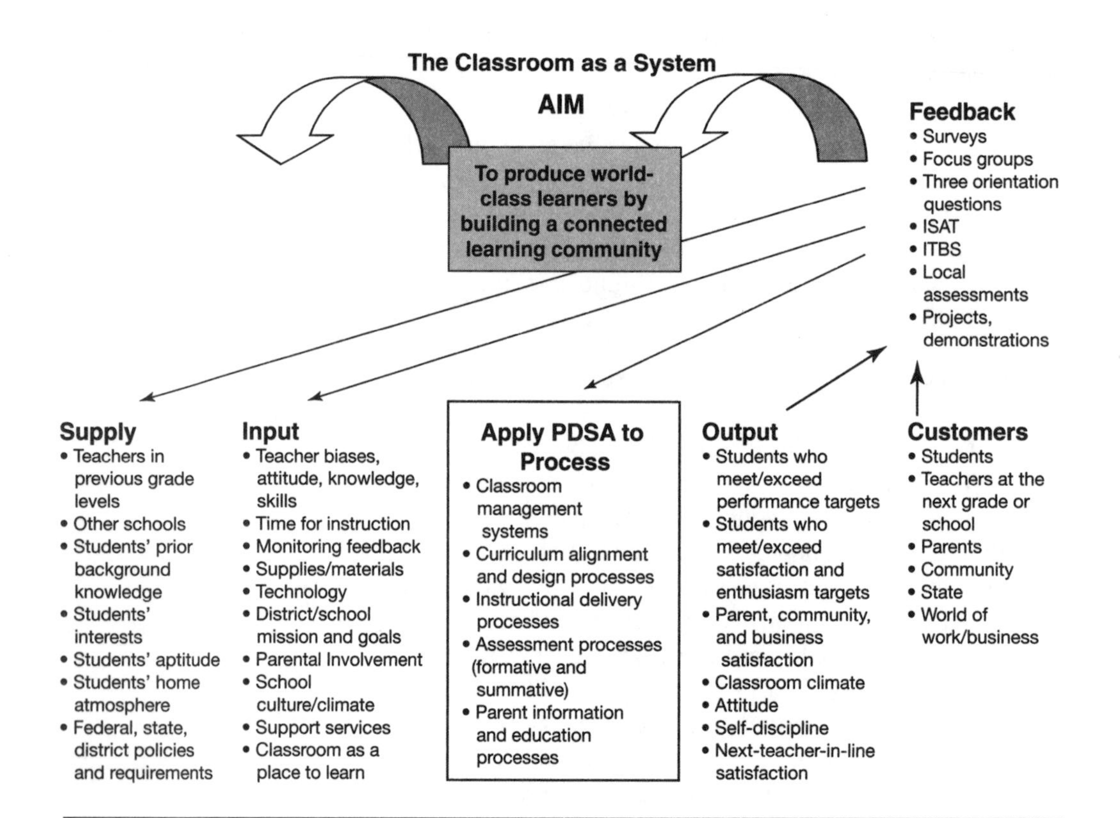

Figure 9.1 System alignment.

clearly understand what students should know and be able to do when they come into the next teacher's classroom. The customer teachers discuss how well they think students are prepared for the next grade or subject level. These same teachers also spend time communicating their own customer requirements to the teachers who supply them with students.

These might not always be comfortable conversations, but they are important ones. If the "supply" of students a teacher receives is not adequately prepared for the next level of learning, the teacher is put at a disadvantage. The teacher not only has the responsibility of teaching the curriculum content for his or her class/grade level, but also at least some of the content from the previous class. When this occurs, it contributes to a widening gap in student achievement as students move through the grades, putting teachers in an incredibly difficult situation. When a teacher has responsibility for teaching students with ability spreads of three, four, or five grades, that means he or she is teaching curriculum content from those grades, a daunting task, and remediating teaching quality issues from previous grades or subject areas. In business, this is called rework and is avoided at all costs, because it does not add value to the product being produced.

This is not an individual teacher issue, it's a classroom, school, and district system issue. Yes, it might be supported or inhibited by the climate of cooperation between professionals in any given school system, but it is part of the classroom system. Teachers cannot be as effective as they want to be unless they clearly define what they want as a customer and what they need from their suppliers. To collect the best feedback, we've scheduled this process for October—after the customer teachers have had an opportunity to evaluate how well students were prepared for their grade level or subject area, if it is in a sequence.

Teachers should audit their classrooms the same way leaders/managers audit their departments and senior leaders audit the district. (See continuous improvement audit questions in "Internal Assessment" section of Chapter 7.) Again, the "How do you know?" question should follow the answer to the audit question to check the depth of understanding about each category. Using the classroom audit questions and the strategic alignment graphic organizer helps teachers to better understand the meaning of the "classroom as a system" and what they can do to continuously improve their system.

If the classroom system is not in alignment, the teacher cannot possibly have an efficient and effective classroom system. If the classroom system is not aligned, the teacher cannot possibly create a learning environment that will help all students be successful. Another way of saying this is that it is possible to have good students, a very smart and professional teacher, good parents, a nice building, a supportive principal, and not have a classroom that works. If elements of a classroom system are misaligned, the classroom can't and won't function well.

Engaging the teaching staff in discussions related to the questions found in the Classroom Orientation to Continuous Improvement and the, "How do you know?" question always provokes thoughtful and useful conversation. For example, ask, "How do you know if your classroom processes are efficient and effective? Who do you ask? What do you ask them? What data do you have to support your assessment of the question?" When classroom processes are efficient and effective, teachers can predict that all students will do well on any test, that students will reach performance targets, that they will spend much less time reteaching, that students will be partners in helping to make decisions about how they want to learn, and students will be enthused about learning. Teachers who think about their classroom as a system consistently get these results. (See the *Continuous Improvement in the Classroom* series published by ASQ for excellent examples of how teachers think about their classrooms as systems.)[5]

As with all other systems, a classroom system is perfectly aligned to get the student results it is getting (behavior as well as academic). If teachers like the results they are getting, then they have aligned the significant processes in the classroom system. If they don't like some of the results they are getting, they will have to realign the classroom system and change the processes within the system they created.

The Student Role in the Classroom System

Helping teachers understand that their classroom is a system is the first step in this instructional revolution. The second step is equally important. This is the step where students become involved in improving the classroom system. One level of conversation about improving the classroom system is between teachers; the second is between the teacher and his or her students.

Continuous improvement requires that we understand how the components of the classroom interact and how teachers and students collaborate to make the classroom system the best it can be for our students. To improve the classroom system, teachers and students need to work together, and they need tools with which to work.

We introduced the PDSA process as a proven method to use for improving results. This process is not an add-on to good instruction, it is a way of assessing and improving good instruction, as demonstrated in every school across our district.

An illustration of student involvement comes from an article, "The News from Room 203," written for parents as a weekly update.

> *The New Year came to Room 203 with a BANG!!!!!!! What an AWESOME first week back after our long and wonderful winter break! We began the week talking about the PDSA cycle. This acronym stands for: Plan, Do, Study, and Act. As a class, we decided that if we could keep our transition times down in between each activity, we could accomplish much more. Our plan was to keep a run chart (graph) of the total transition time lost each day in seconds. We have now done this for the week and have been studying daily what is happening in our classroom. We have been tallying what type of things are increasing our transition times and (the students) are well aware of the acts that we now have to perform. Our goal was to complete each day with less than 5 minutes/300 seconds lost. I'm proud to report from Room 203 that we have been below this 300 seconds four out of five days this week. The kids are also proud of themselves. They are seeing that with more time, we can learn more.*

Where you see good teaching, you see these practices being used by teacher and students. They are the same practices used by thousands of successful teachers and other professionals in businesses across the nation.

Quality Tools in the Classroom

Students can't be good learners without the tools to succeed. Elaine McClanahan in her book, *Future Force*, describes quality tools as the tools that help kids learn.[6] That has been

NAVIGATIONAL TOOLS MAY CONSIST OF CHART INSTRUMENTS, COMPASS, PENCIL, RULER, GPS, AND EVEN RADAR. ACCURACY, RELIABILITY, AND ACCESSIBILITY OF QUALITY NAVIGATION TOOLS IS ESSENTIAL. A 5° STEERING ERROR CAN PUT YOU FIVE MILES OFF COURSE OVER A 60-MILE PASSAGE.

–*SAIL MAGAZINE, JULY 2003, P. 24*

the experience of teachers in our district. Quality tools are thinking tools that help us teach our students 21st century skills like reasoning, problem solving, decision-making, and critical thinking. Quality tools give students the techniques they need to sort through information and make it meaningful. They help them apply what they already know to new and complex situations. And, just as important, quality tools can also help students understand how to be responsible and accountable learners. Without these indispensable tools, students are, as Cleary and Duncan state, "mired in the 20th century."[7] When quality tools are appropriately used in the classroom, teachers can close the gap in students' ability to reason, problem solve, make decisions, think critically, and be responsible for their own learning.

We have developed a Quality Quick Sheet as a quick "tool" reference (see Figure 9.2 and Table 9.1). The front is an organizer that helps teachers decide which tools work best for different purposes, and the back describes the tools in greater detail. We also give a Koalaty Kid Pocket Tools book to each grade level or subject area in each school.

Teaching about and using quality tools with our students is preparing them to be successful and skilled adults who can solve complex problems and make important decisions. There are other things we do that translate to what adults use in their professional lives, but this is one of the most obvious. One easy conclusion we can make about the use of quality tools is that if we help students learn how to use the tools, we are helping them to become successful and competent adults. This is a nice feeling.

The biggest problem we faced was the question of how to provide professional growth experiences teaching the use of quality tools in the classroom to more than 900 certified staff without enough trainers, time, or resources. We solved this problem by having principals and teachers who had used the tools co-present the use of tools in the classroom, thus giving all staff members the same language, information, and skills at the same time. District staff prepared the training materials in short modules so that building staff meeting time could be used to deliver the training. This approach put principals in the role of teaching teachers (not a bad thing) and gave both teachers and principals the same ability to use the tools in the classroom (a very good thing). A scan, where principals visited each classroom to record the use of quality tools, found that 93 percent of our teachers use tools. The most frequently

If you want to:	Expand your thinking	Gather ideas	Group ideas	Connect ideas	Sequence steps	Draw a picture of data	Track facts	Get group consensus	Solve problems and make decisions
These tools may be helpful:	Brain-storming	Affinity diagram	Affinity diagram	Fishbone diagram	Flowchart	Histogram	Check sheet	Light voting	PDSA
	Brain-writing	Brain-storming	Fishbone diagram	Relations diagram	Action plan	Run chart	Line graph	Nominal group technique	Force field
	Nominal group technique	Lotus diagram	Lotus diagram	Radar		Pareto diagram		Censogram	Fishbone diagram
	Affinity diagram	Check-sheet	Consenso-gram	Scatter diagram		Radar			Radar
		Survey				Control chart			Pareto diagram
		Question-naire							Tree diagram
		Focus group							Decision matrix
		Interview							
		Issue bin							

Figure 9.2 Quality quick sheet.

used tools were those used to gather ideas such as the affinity diagram, lotus diagram, issue bin, and brainstorming; to draw a picture of the data tools such as a run chart, Pareto diagram, and radar chart; to solve problems and make decisions such as PDSA, force field, fishbone diagram, and decision matrix; and to connect ideas such as a relations diagram and scattergram.

When our teachers talk about using quality tools in their schools and classrooms, the quotes sound like this:

- "Prompts more professional conversations."
- "Parents are pleased."
- "Better-informed teaching decisions."
- "Kids now track their own data."
- "Students are goal-oriented."
- "Kids decide which quality tools to use—and choose them well."
- "Students have become better problem solvers."

Data-Based Decision-Making in the Classroom

Seemingly, everyone has expectations of a teacher. Students and parents have specific needs and expectations. The next teacher in line expects the teacher to take the right tack in fulfilling his or her role in successfully preparing students. The district has expectations about what the teacher teaches and how well the students perform. All these expectations require the teacher to develop a feedback system that monitors these expectations and gives him or her the information needed to determine if expectations are being met or exceeded. Here's what that system might include:

First, the teacher should want to know exactly what the district expects of him or her in terms that are understandable

Table 9.1 Quality quick sheet.

Quality Tool	Description
Affinity diagram	Relationship or similarity; brainstormed ideas are sorted into categories that have a relationship to each other. Good for assessing prior knowledge, vocabulary awareness, or concept attainment.
Bar chart	Visual display of data; also called histogram; can be a Pareto diagram.
Brainstorming	Used to generate a large number of ideas in a short period of time. Participants call out ideas—no evaluation or judgement should be made-all ideas are recorded.
Brainwriting	Nonverbal brainstorming when team members write ideas on sheets of paper, then exchange papers and write more ideas.
Cause-and-effect chart	See Fishbone diagram.
Check sheet	Tool to organize data collection. Often organized in rows or columns, with data occurrences checked off or tallied.
Consensogram	Used to identify knowledge or opinions of a group on certain concepts or issues.
Decision matrix	Used to help people see the value of individual components involved in a decision.
Fishbone diagram	Helps discern contributing factors to an outcome or problem. Also know as cause-and-effect diagrams. Causes are recorded on the bones of the fish-effect in the head. Also used to develop whole-part relationships, and so on novel elements, event and elements that contributed to it.
Flowchart	Visual documentation of a process. Shows step-by-step approach to a specific process by using symbols to denote tasks, decisions, and stages. Can be general process or deployment (specific roles assigned to tasks).
Focus group	Type of survey—used to gather attitudes and concerns from a small group, usually randomly selected. Interviewer takes notes on responses.
Force-field analysis	A problem-solving tool used to analyze driving and restraining forces that surround a proposed change.
Histogram	Bar chart that provides visual representation of data. Bars are arranged in order with respect to time, size, volume, and so on.
Interview	Type of survey—used to gather open-ended responses, either face-to-face or by phone, from a small group.
Issue bin	Captures ideas/questions that deserve further clarification or discussion at a later or more appropriate time. Also called bin or parking lot.
Light voting	Way to determine consensus by allowing team members to cast weighted votes to designate items with their greatest support. Total number of points for a item determines which item to choose. Related to nominal group technique.
Line graph	Also known as run chart.
Lotus diagram	Organizes and breaks down broad topics into components. Done on folded paper - nine squares. Each of the exterior squares can be further broken down into nine subtopic squares (called a mega lotus).
Nominal group technique	Way to determine consensus by allowing team members to cast weighted votes to designate their greatest support. Total number of "hits" an item gets (not weight of vote) determines items to choose. Related to light voting.
Pareto diagram	A bar chart giving a visual representation of data in order of its frequency (greatest to least). Highest bar represents priority action item.
PDSA cycle	Plan-Do-Study-Act, a cycle that reflects continuous improvement. Uses the scientific method in relation to systemic improvement and problem solving.
Questionnaire	Type of survey—used to collect data from a large group. Can be open response (short answers) or based on a continuum form negative to positive.
Radar	Gives a picture of the strengths and weaknesses of a system. Performance is rated on spokes around a hub. Points are connected to form a visual interpretation of results.
Relations diagram	A pictorial representation of the cause-and-effect relationships among elements of a problem or issue.
Run chart	A line graph of data plotted over time.
Scatter diagram	Graph showing the relationship between two factors. The pattern formed by the plotted dots help to analyze causes and indicates if a true relationship exists.
Survey	Used to collect knowledge/opinions of a targeted group. Can be written, phone, or face-to-face. Used to discover customers' views (external and internal) of supplier's performance.
Tree diagram	Identifies actions to solve a problem or implement a solution. Moves thinking from broad goals to specifics. Answers the question: How can this be accomplished?

and measurable. We say "should" because this is not always something a teacher wants to know or seeks out. The answer to an expectations question brings with it a clear indication of accountability. As long as outcomes are ill defined and measures or targets are lacking, then whatever is achieved is good enough. Remember, you are fighting an accountability culture clash.

It is important to note that it is not the teacher's responsibility to define these measures or targets; it is a senior leadership responsibility. We would assume they reflect the expectations of parents and the community. Teachers would certainly be involved in the strategic planning process and in setting curriculum standards and benchmarks, but setting and communicating performance expectations is a primary responsibility of leaders in the organization. This is an extremely important piece of the student performance puzzle, and one that if solved, truly transforms a classroom, a school, or a district. The Student Performance Targets described in Chapter 7 are examples of measurable expectations and are certainly the expectations on which we want our teachers to focus.

Another approach to expectations can be a teacher skill or behavior list using various standards documents (state professional teacher standards, the National Board for Professional Teaching Standards, and so on). Using state professional teacher standards (content knowledge, human development and learning, diversity, planning for instruction, learning environment, instructional delivery, communication, assessment, collaborative relationships, reflection and professional growth, professional conduct), we have described specific behaviors in each category that our teachers must master by the end of their second year of employment in our district. The mastery of these behaviors is a condition of further employment and the awarding of tenure. Our responsibility is to design and deploy staff development programs that address deficit areas in each of the professional teacher standards, so that newly hired teachers have the support to master the prescribed behaviors.

We described the standardized process teachers use to collect expectations from parents at the start of the school year. Many teachers also put those expectations on their Web pages and report progress in meeting those expectations in class newsletters and other communications. Teachers monitor these parent expectations throughout the year and give an end-of-year report about how well they were accomplished.

TACK: TO PROGRESS FROM POINT A TO POINT B BY MAKING A SERIES OF MOVES THAT REFLECT A STRATAGEM. A VESSEL SAILING AGAINST THE WIND TRAVELS FORWARD BY MAKING A SERIES OF ZIGZAG MOVEMENTS. THAT PROCESS, CALLED TACKING, REQUIRES CHANGING THE POSITION OF THE SAILS TO ALTER THE DIRECTION OF THE SHIP ... METAPHORICALLY, A PERSON IS ON THE WRONG TACK WHEN TAKING THE WRONG APPROACH TO A SITUATION OR AN ISSUE. TO CORRECT THE ERROR AND TAKE THE RIGHT TACK, THE COURSE OF ACTION MUST BE ALTERED.

—*WHEN A LOOSE CANNON FLOGS A DEAD HORSE THERE'S THE DEVIL TO PAY, P. 98*

Expectations for student satisfaction and enthusiasm for learning are monitored a number of ways. Student satisfaction often is included as a part of the SIP and is therefore monitored by in-process measures throughout the year. These data are used at staff meetings and grade-level meetings to determine if improvements are working.

Student enthusiasm for learning is monitored using a Class Fast Feedback Form and an Enthusiasm vs. Learning Survey. (We give all the credit to Jeffrey J. Burgard for this survey, found in his book, *Continuous Improvement in the Science Classroom*.[8]) We have bought multiple copies of the Continuous Improvement Series by Fauss, Ayres, and Carson and find them to be exceptional resources to show how expectations are monitored in the classroom.[9] Teachers use the Class Fast Feedback Form periodically at the end of a lesson to get feedback about how well the lesson was received. The form is used in third grade and above; simpler versions are used in first and second grade.

The Enthusiasm vs. Learning Survey tells teachers at a glance how a class feels about a subject or unit of study at its completion. Students place an adhesive dot on a poster or transparency at the point where their two feelings meet (for example, "learned a lot" and "liked it"). The class goal should be to see an increase in the concentration of dots in the upper-right quadrant, which are student statements about what they liked and what suggestions they have for improvement. After posting their dots, students also complete a plus delta about the unit or have a discussion about why they placed the dot where they did and what class improvements it might suggest. Student ideas are tallied and used by the teacher when designing a new unit of study. Classrooms use this as trend data, change what is possible using the PDSA cycle, and inform students about what is not possible to change (see Figure 9.3).

We have been collecting enthusiasm data in the way described by Lee Jenkins in the first edition of his book, *Improving Student Learning*, but setting an organizational goal (Student Performance Target) for learning enthusiasm was not enough.[10] Our data suggested that each grade level attained by students contributed to the demise of their enthusiasm for learning. That is, the slope of the data started in the 90 percent area for all subjects in kindergarten, but by eighth grade it was only in the 20 and 30 percent area for all subjects, except for physical education and art. This trend data

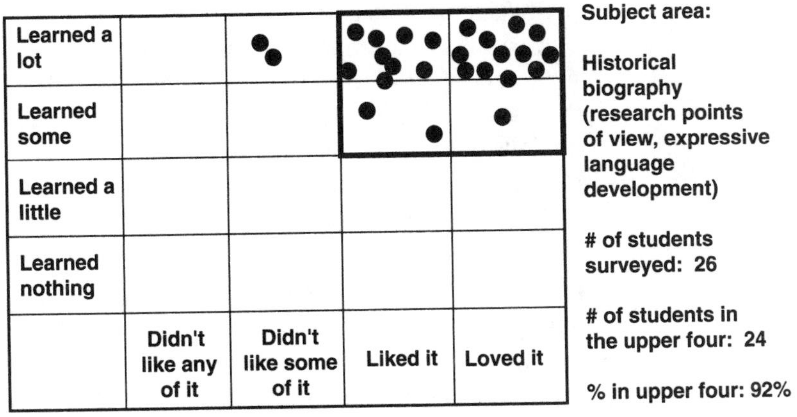

Learned a lot				
Learned some				
Learned a little				
Learned nothing				
	Didn't like any of it	Didn't like some of it	Liked it	Loved it

Subject area:

Historical biography (research points of view, expressive language development)

# of students surveyed: 26

# of students in the upper four: 24

% in upper four: 92%

Figure 9.3 Student enthusiasm vs. learning.

continued for a few years until we finally asked ourselves whether we were satisfied with this result or if we wanted to do something about it. We chose to take action, and identified the lack of active participation by students in improving enthusiasm for learning as the root cause for this problem.

Teachers began to use the Enthusiasm vs. Learning Survey as an in-process measure, and schools set goals for learning enthusiasm in their SIPs. The results? In third grade, enthusiasm for reading improved by 50 percent, and in fifth and eighth grades, by 100 percent. We were continuing to learn the lesson that the only way to get performance improvement was through the use of in-process measures. It is a simple lesson, but it took us much too long to learn it.

One last word about expectations and feedback. We agree with the distinction that Lee Jenkins makes about the goals of teaching, that is, teachers should design instruction so that students remember, not forget.[11] His assertion is that most instruction is designed to give permission to students to forget. He also suggests that teachers should collect three types of classroom data:

1. Information (the number of things like facts, episodes, concepts, generalizations/principles, operations, algorithms, and time sequences students know vs. what they should know, collected weekly)
2. Level of enthusiasm for learning
3. Knowledge (the ability to apply the information students know, collected at the end of a unit)

We confess that we have not found ways to convince all our teachers to teach in ways that help students to remember, not forget, and to collect the types of classroom in-process data that really make a difference in student learning. This is an obvious opportunity for improvement.

What we have found through the clarification of expectations and the use of new feedback processes is that students who feel ownership of the classroom and key processes (because they have had a hand in shaping them) become more eager and enthusiastic to learn and work cooperatively. Students are learning more and learning it faster, and less reteaching is required. These are not insignificant accomplishments.

After all, isn't this what teachers want? Isn't this what teachers hoped to achieve when they entered this profession? Isn't this what we all want to work together to achieve? We know what to do. What we need is to continue to support each other in thinking about and trying to understand how considering the classroom as a system can help to accomplish this.

This completes our journey through this complex system called education. We have stopped at many ports and shared our reactions as travelers on this continuous improvement adventure. We have a few more observations and conclusions we want to share with you in the last chapter. The voyage is not quite over.

ENDNOTES

1. Saunders, William L., and Sandra P. Horn. 1998. *Teacher effectiveness and student achievement: Findings resulting from Tennessee value-added assessment system data analyses.* Knoxville, TN: University of Tennessee, Value-Added Research and Assessment Center
2. Ibid.
3. Marzano, Robert. 2003. *What works in schools: Translating research into action*. Alexandria, VA: ASCD.
4. Haycock, Kati, Craig Jerald, and Sandra Huang. 2001. Closing the gap: Done in a decade. *Thinking K-16*, (Spring): 5.
5. Ayres, Carolyn. Shelly C. Carson, Karen R. Fauss. 2000. *ASQ continuous improvement series*. Milwaukee: ASQ Quality Press.
6. McClanahan, Elaine, and Carolyn Wicks. 1993. *Future force*. Chino Hills, CA: Pact Publishing.

7. Cleary, Barbara A. and Sally J. Duncan. 1999. *Thinking tools for kids: An activity book for classroom learning.* Milwaukee: ASQ Quality Press.
8. Burgard, Jeffrey J. 2000. *Continuous improvement in the science classroom.* Milwaukee: ASQ Quality Press.
9. Ayres, Carolyn. Shelly C. Carson, Karen R. Fauss. 2000. *ASQ continuous improvement series*, Milwaukee: ASQ Quality Press.
10. Jenkins, Lee. 2003. *Improving student learning*, 2nd edition. Milwaukee: ASQ Quality Press.
11. Ibid.

10

Navigating the Future of Organizational Excellence: Developing and Sustaining the Continuous Improvement Culture

At the beginning of this book, we suggested that you read it as you would a case study, because that was our intent in writing it. Our purpose was to keep your thinking about whole system improvement grounded in the real context of a school district story. When a case study is written effectively, you gather insights as you read about how to address similar situations in your own organization, and you strategize about how you could use the examples more effectively to create even better results. If you have read the book in this manner, then we have successfully accomplished our purpose. There remains just one final activity: to compare your thoughts and our suggestions about additional changes that could help our organizations improve and enable us to achieve the student and staff goals that are the sign of a great school district. No matter where your organization is on the deployment continuum, these suggestions should help.

Suggestions for Senior Leaders

In Chapter 4, we recommended four steps for senior leaders who are seeking to position (or align) their organizations for excellence. Here are a few more thoughts about these steps.

Our experience leads us to stress the point that a good beginning requires a focused, clear strategic plan developed with broad stakeholder input as we described in Chapter 3.

Starting with a broad base of constituent participation means that senior leaders can talk about the mission, vision, and goals that have been developed by the community and staff, not ones that came from administrators or a select group of people who come together, isolate themselves for a couple of days, and emerge with a plan. Without being able to reference the goals as belonging to the community and staff, senior leaders have a much harder time focusing people in the organization on what goals need to be accomplished, what effort it will take to accomplish them, and what resources are necessary if they are to be accomplished. *We can't overemphasize the leverage senior leaders have with this shift in who owns the strategic plan.*

Using the Baldrige criteria as the framework for continuous improvement activities requires aligning your organization to the Baldrige framework. As we discussed in Chapter 3, that is possible only when you have established a strong set of core values, key goals, and both leading and lagging measures for those goals. In Chapter 2, we noted that Baldrige is a means to an end, not the end in itself. Continuous improvement is the means senior leaders use to accomplish the ends, the goals of the organization. Without measurable goals, what will you aim for? What will your target be? Even if you have a strategic plan, we would suggest it conform to the recommendations made in Chapter 3.

With a strategic plan that shows a clear direction or aim, senior leaders need to speak with one voice when discussing the use of the Baldrige criteria as the framework for continuous improvement activities. To unify your leaders' voices, we recommend what we call an executive coaching experience (generally two days in length) as a forum for a frank and open discussion about what it takes to create a quality educational organization. That discussion, we think, should include developing answers to these eight questions:

1. What does adopting the Baldrige framework mean to an organization?
2. What roles and responsibilities will we need to individually and collectively assume if we use the Baldrige framework?
3. What will it take to successfully adopt the Baldrige framework into our organization?

4. What is necessary to develop and maintain Baldrige-based strategic and short- and longer-term action plans?
5. How can we best practice continuous improvement?
6. What training and involvement would be most effective for senior leaders, board members, and department staff?
7. What would a workable deployment timeline look like?
8. What are the best approaches to implement timeline activities?

One of the first outcomes from this discussion should be a set of talking points for the superintendent and his or her direct reports to use when describing the Baldrige framework to constituent groups both inside and outside the organization so that everything is above board. It is essential to come to a common understanding about how the Baldrige framework will be used and what responses will be given to questions that are asked. When someone asks, "Isn't this just a business model?" or states, "This is just another administrator fad we don't need!" there must be a similar response, no matter which senior leader is answering. More importantly, you need common language about how the Baldrige framework and criteria can be used to help the organization improve, and answers can't be vague or general. Examples, flowcharts, timelines, and action plans need to be available and referenced when answering the "How does this work?" and "How will this affect me?" type of questions.

Above Board—Literally the wooden boards of planking which make up the deck. Any activity which went on "above boards" would be in the open for everyone to see. Thus it has come to mean honest and fair dealing.
–*Salty Dog Talk*, p. 5

Senior leaders have to gain the confidence of key staff and community members at the beginning of the adoption of a new change management framework (another description of the Baldrige criteria) if it is to succeed. When senior leaders are secure and united in their understanding of the what, why, when, where, and how of Baldrige, staff and community members will have more confidence. If there is a perception of confusion or disharmony at the top of the organization, the staff and community will not sign on, and you will have missed the opportunity to create a good first impression. Now you understand why two days is the minimum amount of time necessary for senior leaders to discuss and think about these questions.

One recommended activity during this two-day executive coaching session is a preliminary audit of each department. Helping senior leaders in the organization experience how applying the Baldrige framework can help them think about their departments as systems and give them the tools to assess system strengths and weaknesses is a very important outcome. This activity provides senior leaders with examples they can use when discussing the Baldrige framework with their staff. It also provides a depth of understanding about the criteria that is so necessary for further deployment.

Senior leaders need some time to consider and discuss how to move systems thinking and self-assessment practices into departments, individual work plans, assessment activities, and then to the school and classroom levels. Thinking it up as you go is not recommended, nor is the "shock and awe" approach. A general deployment plan should emerge from this initial executive coaching session with details filled in with the assistance of staff as the timeline moves ahead.

Another recommendation includes encouraging senior leaders to become state quality program or state award examiners. We have found no better training for understanding and applying the Baldrige criteria than taking a case study of an organization and identifying strengths and opportunities for improvement. We have a requirement that all senior leaders and principals have to become state examiners, and we recommend this step to aspiring administrators as well. Administrators who are in doctoral programs have said they have not studied harder than when they became state examiners, and some will surely complain. And, even though the commitment of time is great, we suggest that the superintendent also become a Baldrige examiner. Expertise does not come easily or cheaply, and leaders need to be seen as experts.

We suggest early training on what are called the "statistical and managerial seven" (see p. 62).These are the continuous quality improvement tools most often used by leaders to analyze quantitative and qualitative data and to facilitate the development of goals, PDSA improvement cycles, and action plans. We have found a strong relationship between the department or school leaders' effectiveness and their knowledge and ability to use these tools.

A good source for training on these tools is the Koalaty Kid training program (see Chapter 6). This program teaches all the previously mentioned tools.

As soon as senior leaders develop an expertise and comfort with the Baldrige framework and criteria, Category Champion teams should be created. We suggested a way to organize these teams in Chapter 4. Senior leaders need to at least co-chair these teams to ensure linkages between categories. Regular senior leader meetings should be devoted to Category Champion team meeting updates and cross linkages between categories.

A communication plan needs to be developed to showcase the "talking points" senior leaders have been rehearsing. Good opportunities include regularly scheduled standing committees (both internal and external) such as the PTA/PTO, curriculum groups, union executive boards, director and coordinators, chambers of commerce, service organizations, and building staff meetings. The goal should be for every staff member in the district and key communicators in the community to hear a senior leader discuss the Baldrige framework and how it can help the people in the organization meet or exceed their professional goals.

Finally, senior leaders need to review department operational definitions (once they have been developed) as described in Chapter 5 and determine what quality characteristics will become part of the department leader's One-Page Plan and which will constitute the district's balanced scorecard. Making these decisions completes the accountability loop and makes it clear to senior leaders and the board of education what improvements the district leaders are holding themselves accountable for and what measures will be used to monitor performance.

KNOW THE ROPES—THE RIGGING IN A LARGE SAILING SHIP COULD COMPRISE UPWARDS OF TEN MILES OF CORDAGE . . . MOST OF THE HAULING ROPES WERE MADE OF THE SAME MATERIAL, A GREAT MANY WERE THE SAME SIZE AND ALMOST ALL WERE OF THE SAME CONSTRUCTION, HENCE IT WAS VERY DIFFICULT TO TELL ONE FROM ANOTHER. ONLY FROM THE PRECISE POSITION THAT ROPES WERE SECURED ON DECK COULD THEY BE IDENTIFIED . . . THE TERM "KNOWING THE ROPES" BECAME THE DISTINCTION BETWEEN THE OLD HAND AND THE BEGINNER.

–SALTY DOG TALK, P. 45

Suggestions for Director or Managerial Level

It is important that directors and managers "know the ropes." They cannot support and implement the Baldrige process if they don't understand the purpose and the importance of it. We suggest a meeting with directors and coordinators of internal and support services before the beginning of the school year. The agenda might look something like this:

1. *Overview of the Baldrige framework as a change management strategy*

   This is the gist of what needs to be said: The ability to manage change should be one of the top priorities for directors and coordinators because this is the operational level where the real work gets done and where improvements are deployed. How well change is managed will determine how well the organization achieves its goals, and most importantly, the quality of education provided to students. Have directors and coordinators pair up to discuss this strategy and then share their discussion with the larger group. This will get discussion moving around these ideas and give the agenda facilitator feedback and reactions.

2. *Continuous improvement self-audit*

   Give directors and coordinators time to complete the seven continuous improvement audit questions. (See Internal Assessment section of Chapter 7). The answers to these questions—or the lack of answers—will be important in the development of operational definitions. Having participants share answers is useful to help clarify the intent of the questions. Be sure to connect the questions to the Baldrige framework, as obvious as it may seem to you. Remind participants that the self-audit they have just completed is the same kind of audit or assessment the district will be using to evaluate alignment issues.

3. *Developing operational definitions*

   The next step is to have the directors/coordinators or managers develop operational definitions based on their audit answers. (This will be problematic if the answers to the audit questions are "I don't know.") Even if they don't know for sure who their customers are and what they want, they should have a good idea or they are in the wrong job. Ask them to build their operational definitions, as described in Chapter 5, based on their best knowledge and experience. Also remember, as we pointed out, operational definition measures should include both leading and lagging indicators.

   If our past experience is any predictor, there will be a reluctance to raise the decision criteria bar. In other words, the meeting facilitator will probably have to encourage participants to "stretch" their thinking about what levels of performance would meet or exceed customer expectations and requirements. They likely will also want to know how this information will be used. The answer is always for helping to move the principles and practices of continuous improvement forward, not to "get" people. This distinction is important if you are to gain trust in using operational definitions as an accountability and improvement strategy.

Operational definitions will have a significant, even profound, impact on your current processes for setting targets (goals), for measuring them over time, and for holding leaders accountable for results. Beyond the development step, adequate time and resources need to be devoted to supporting and assisting directors/coordinators as they make that change.

4. *Developing or refining job descriptions aligned to operational definitions*

   In the memo inviting directors and coordinators to this meeting, they should be asked to bring job descriptions for all staff positions under their leadership. Each job description should be reviewed with the operational definitions in mind. Do the job descriptions reflect what the operational definitions say is important for that employee or group of employees to know and accomplish? If operational definitions and job descriptions are not aligned, they need to be rewritten and the process should begin at this meeting.

5. *Developing or refining job targets aligned to operational definitions*

   Next, ask the directors/coordinators/managers to align job targets. Job targets, in this case, mean the numerical targets that you want to accomplish over a period of time. It is the act of thinking about progress attained and yet to be achieved, and then determining improvements that would be a "stretch" and setting a timeline to accomplish them. Directors/coordinators/managers need time to think and discuss how they will convey the targets to staff, especially if staff members have not worked under

STANDARD OPERATING PROCEDURE (S.O.P.)—WE MUST ACCEPT THE FACT THAT SYSTEMS AND PROCEDURES PLAY AN IMPORTANT ROLE IN BEING SKIPPER OF A SAILBOAT. IN THE SHORT RUN, TAKING EVERY STEP THE SAME WAY AND WITH THE SAME ROUTINE WILL SAVE TIME AND WORRY ... IN THE LONG RUN, ESTABLISHING AND FOLLOWING ALIGNMENT OF PROCEDURES WILL SAVE MISTAKES, AND PERHAPS A DISASTER ... INSTRUCTIONS AND REPORTS ABOUT COURSES AND BEARINGS MUST BE CLEARLY ENUNCIATED BY THE SPEAKER AND ACKNOWLEDGED BY THE LISTENER ... MORE BOATS HAVE GOTTEN INTO TROUBLE DUE TO POOR COMMUNICATIONS THAN TO BAD PILOTING.

–*THE ANNAPOLIS BOOK OF SEAMANSHIP, P. 242*

targets in the past. They will have to persuade staff members who might not view an increased responsibility and performance accountability as a good thing. We have found the custodian story in Chapter 5 a useful example during this discussion.

6. *Developing or refining job performance evaluations aligned to operational definitions*

   Job performance evaluations are usually negotiated, so changing them will likely not happen during this meeting. However, directors/coordinators need to assess the alignment or agreement (or lack thereof) between operational definitions, job descriptions, and job evaluations. If there isn't alignment between them, you can't expect staff members to clearly understand their jobs or what their contributions to the organization are. Job evaluations that don't align to job descriptions and operational definitions are, from our point of view, a waste of time and a lost opportunity for improvement. This agenda item will raise issues, but they are issues that need to be discussed. If necessary, alignment steps need to be designed.

7. *Developing staff training priorities and activities aligned to operational definitions and job descriptions*

   The last alignment step at this meeting is to have the directors and coordinators review their operational definition targets in relation to current levels of performance and to look at the revised job descriptions to determine what skills and abilities are the most important for staff to develop and apply. At least a brief outline of activities to accomplish these training priorities should be designed at this time.

We declared our alignment mantra earlier in the book. This agenda is an example of that mantra in action. It is the kind of alignment that must go on throughout the organization if significant improvements in performance are to be achieved.

At the next meeting with directors/coordinators/managers, the agenda would be devoted to debriefing reactions to the department operational definitions as presented at staff meetings— a "This is what they said" and "This is how I responded" kind of session. After a time for debriefing, the directors and coordinators should start building PDSAs. The PDSA form in Chapter 6 is the one we use for this activity. If "stretch" decision criteria were set, there certainly should be some opportunities for improvement. We have also included examples of completed PDSAs in the Appendix A because examples are always helpful when learning a new tool or process.

Change management knowledge and skill development for directors and coordinators will be ongoing agenda items, as will continual refinements of operational definitions and PDSA cycles of improvement. For example, if participants do not have confirming evidence that clearly describes customer expectations and requirements, a PDSA could be developed for designing an approach to gathering this information. If there is a need to develop methods for leading or lagging data gathering and analysis, this could become a PDSA. (As we mentioned earlier, if drastic improvement is needed, benchmarking, not PDSA, would be the preferred change management strategy.)

Suggestions for Principals

The principals' role is to lead the School Improvement Process as we described in Chapter 8. However, we found it difficult to enlist principals' committed participation until we had developed the SIP flowchart that described activities, and information needs, and provided the forms that have to be filled out at each step—along with the calendar that described monthly SIP activities. Making data instantly available using the electronic data warehouse was a big plus.

What really made the difference for us was another alignment issue—aligning principal evaluations to SIP goals. This makes great sense, because principals, as they should, pay close attention to issues addressed in their performance reviews. When we designed the performance review based on a self-assessment of progress made related to SIP goals, we put the focus of principal performance where it should be. To help them understand what is important, we developed discussion questions like these for their evaluation conferences:

- Which processes in your school have the highest priority for improvement? What data led you and your staff to this conclusion and most influenced your choices about which goals to focus on in your SIP?

- Describe your outcome statements and why you think they "stretch" your staff yet are still realistic to achieve?
- What are your process performance measures? Do the data (quantitative and/or qualitative) make you believe you will achieve your goals for this year? Are the measures used frequently enough to accurately assess the effectiveness of your improvement efforts?
- Which Student Performance Targets are you most concerned about achieving by 2005?
- What do you believe is necessary to accomplish to achieve those targets by 2005?
- What systems alignment issues cause you the greatest concern? What do we need to do to overcome these alignment issues?
- How well is PDSA being used in your school? In classrooms? What examples of its use would you share to help us understand the process better?
- From the summary of the Baldrige audit your staff did of the school, how have you and your staff monitored the "vital few" improvements over time and what are your results?

One more suggestion. If you haven't already tried this, have principals make presentations to the board of education, individually or in groups, that describe the goals they are working to achieve and how those goals align to the accomplishment of the district's mission. The board needs to know how school improvement goals are aligned to the district mission, and in a general way, what the schools are doing to address performance improvement.

Suggestions for Teachers and Staff

In the beginning, we were least effective in deploying the principles and practices of continuous quality improvement at the classroom level. We tried several things that just didn't work as well as we wanted.

First, we created "demonstration teachers" in each school who would open their doors so that any other teacher could come in and see how quality tools are used with students to improve classroom practice and results. Great idea, few visits.

Next, a parade of outside experts worked with groups of teachers to develop skills in applying quality tools in the classroom and to help principals understand the benefits of requiring teachers to use continuous improvement practices. Some interest, little implementation.

We then tried a teacher on special assignment. This "star" had transformed her classroom by using quality tools with her students. She was enthusiastic and effective one on one, but with one teacher as teacher and 900 teachers as students, deployment using that strategy would have taken us between five and ten years.

All these approaches worked to a degree and helped to get out the word about a new way to think about student/teacher collaboration to improve instruction, but they weren't fast enough or as effective as they needed to be.

We thought about the Baldrige Category 1 sequence in which senior leaders set, communicate, and deploy goals and performance expectations, and decided that principals would be the ideal trainers. We developed four training modules that principals would use to convey the theory and application of continuous quality improvement in the classroom:

- The first helped to create an understanding about the practical application of the Baldrige framework to classroom practice. The audit questions found in Chapter 7 served as the organizer for that module.
- The second module taught the use of the quality tools found in the Quality Quick Sheet shown in Chapter 9. The focus of the training was the concept of active student involvement in classroom decisions as well as student responsibility for setting goals and monitoring attainment using quality tools.
- The third module addressed the application of the PDSA cycle as the method of significantly improving classroom practice and results, again with student participation. (The most effective instructor for teaching the PDSA cycle was a fifth-grade student we captured on videotape. She knew exactly what PDSA was and how to use it.)

- The last module taught teachers to see their classroom as a system and how to think systematically about designing and delivering effective classroom instruction.

The Teacher and Student Partnerships Train-the-Trainer materials developed by Jim Shipley and Associates,[1] *Quality Fusion* and other materials developed by Margaret Byrnes and Robert Cornesky,[2] and the *Total Quality Transformation Exercises, Keys, and Forms: Education K-12*, developed by PQ Systems[3] were particularly useful resources as we developed these four modules.

The advantage of this deployment approach proved to be that principals had to develop expertise in each area. They were viewed as teachers of teachers, not a usual role for principals. Another advantage is that all 900 teachers were trained in the same content at the same time, usually during staff meetings—a highly effective use of staff meeting time as well as a means for ensuring consistency of our message.

We are working on two additional modules that grew out of our continuing discussions with staff and principals. One focuses on data-based decision making and the other on student involvement in the learning process.

You noticed the supplier-customer chain displayed in the "Classroom as a System" (Figure 9.1) in Chapter 9. A parent expectations survey (the three questions at the beginning of Chapter 9) is something we strongly recommend you implement across your district. It is an important first step that helps teachers make the transition to thinking about their classrooms as systems and become more aware that the classroom is there to satisfy customer needs and expectations. One caution: there needs to be an expectation that teachers will follow up on the information received from parents throughout the year. The survey needs to be positioned not as an event, but as one component of an ongoing classroom systems perspective.

A related idea is to create an expectation that teachers meet with other teachers in supplier-customer roles to exchange feedback and expectations about student performance. In our experience, this results in a powerful change in perspective, and the feedback prompts immediate changes in classroom practice.

Final Thoughts

"If not you, who? If not now, when?"—Anonymous

We have pointed out how important it is to develop a "no excuses" culture. As senior leaders, we are the people responsible for where we are now, and we are responsible for getting to a better place in the future. We have to have the courage to admit we have to do better, because we cannot fail our students. We must step forward and acknowledge that we are good, but we are not great—and that's not good enough!

We don't think all this means that we should strive to become the instruments of earth-shattering change *only*. Our perspective and experience indicate that small improvements are just fine. We don't need to solve everything at once. But we do have to get started.

We have come a long way together in the pages of this book. We have looked at the Baldrige framework as a powerful change management strategy for improving any organization, whether that organization is a district, a school, or a classroom. We have demonstrated why leadership is the first category of the Baldrige criteria and why it is vital to successful application of the Baldrige or any other change management strategies.

We have suggested a flow of steps that will create a powerful deployment plan for moving your organization and culture to the next level and given you some easily customized tools to use along the way. We have shown that it is necessary for these steps to be completed (or at least well deployed) at the district level before moving the principles and practices of continuous improvement to the school or classroom level.

Now it's up to you. We are sure you work in schools that have established a proud heritage. You are in an enviable position of being able to build on a strong reputation of performance. We congratulate you not only on all your impressive past achievements, but also on your desire not to say "good enough." It is clear that you are ready to forge a new chapter of greatness for your students, your staff, and your community. We hope that this book will help you write that new chapter for your organization.

TO ENJOY SAILING … YOU MUST TRY TO STANDARDIZE YOUR TECHNIQUES AND YOUR EQUIPMENT AND DO EVERY JOB THE SAME WAY, TIME AFTER TIME. ALWAYS USE EITHER MAGNETIC OR TRUE DEGREES. ALWAYS ACKNOWLEDGE A COMMAND. ALWAYS TAKE EVERY OPPORTUNITY TO FIX YOUR POSITION. ALWAYS STOP THE BOAT'S FORWARD MOTION WHEN A CREWMEMBER FALLS OVERBOARD. ALWAYS GAUGE THE BOAT'S PERFORMANCE BY HER BALANCE. WITH REPETITION COMES GOOD HABITS, WITH GOOD HABITS COMES GOOD SEAMANSHIP, WITH GOOD SEAMANSHIP COMES SECURITY, AND WITH SECURITY COMES SUCCESS AND COMPLETION OF YOUR JOURNEY.

–THE ANNAPOLIS BOOK OF SEAMANSHIP, P. 375

ENDNOTES

1. Shipley, Jim. 2001. *The teacher and student partnerships train-the-trainer.* Seminole, FL: Jim Shipley & Associates.
2. Byrnes, Margaret A., and Robert A. Cornesky. 1994. *Quality fusion: Turning total quality management into classroom practice*. Anderson, SC: Cornesky & Associates, Inc.
3. *Total quality transformation: Exercises, keys, and forms: Education (K-12)*. 1995. Miamisburg, OH: PQ Systems, Inc.

Appendix A

Category Champion Teams (September 24, 2001)

The Baldrige criteria provide a systems perspective that assists in informing the management of District 15 how to achieve performance excellence. We have clearly defined what achieving performance excellence means in Strategic Vision 2005. The key goals in that document have been given further clarification and direction by the District 15 Board of Education Goals and the Student Performance Targets. Successful management of District 15 requires that all functions of the organization be aligned if we are to achieve performance excellence. Alignment includes a focus on our mission and key goals; the board goals and related student performance targets; strategic directions and plans; monitoring, responding to, and managing all operations; using measures/indicators to link key strategies for improvement with processes; and making sure resources are prioritized and distributed so that overall performance and student and stakeholder satisfaction improves.

Category Teams are a powerful strategy for increasing ownership in the principles and practices of continuous improvement. The purpose of Category Teams is to be responsible for the approach and deployment of the criteria related to an individual category and to review data and suggest improvements within that category. Category Teams generally have two co-champions or co-chairs and from seven to eleven team members, plus an advisor who is on call to the team. The Category Teams meet three times and use data and documents already available within the organization to review progress and suggest changes as part of the continuous improvement process. The teams assure clarification of what the criteria mean, assess gaps in approach and deployment, translate the gap analysis into actionable improvements, link across categories, and chart progress.

Category Team Membership

Category 1: (Superintendent and CTC president, co-champions). Team members would include a board member, two or three principals, two teachers, one support staff member, and a PTA representative.

Category 2: DACEE would serve as the category team.

Category 3: (Director of communications and a CTC executive board member, co-champions). Teams members would be the same as category 1.

Category 4: (Directory of planning and a CTC executive board member). Team members would be the same as category 1.

Category 5: (Assistant superintendent for personnel and human services and a CTC executive board member). Team members would be the same as category 1.

Category 6: (Assistant superintendent for instructional and special services, the executive director to the superintendent for administrative services, the assistant superintendent for business and auxiliary services and a CTC executive board member). Team members would be the same as category 1.

Category 7: Each Category Team 1-6 would be responsible for the results of its category in category 7.

Category Team Meeting Times

Suggested meeting times could be in early November, January, and March. Teams need to allot three hours per meeting to adequately accomplish their agendas.

Category Team Meeting Agendas

October:

- Membership invitations sent with 2001 Education Criteria for Performance Excellence books and the Organizational Profile (*expectation that the criteria for the category and the Organizational Profile be read before the first meeting*).
- Gather data that are currently available related to your category (*your advisor may be helpful here*).
- Plan for the first meeting with your co-champion (*your advisor may be helpful here*). [NOTE: District 15 had three internal Baldrige criteria experts, but an advisor could be either internal or external to the organization.]

November Team Meeting:

- Introductions and overview of the purpose of Category Teams.
- Discuss category criteria and answer questions (*your advisor may be useful here*).
- Discuss the Organizational Profile and answer questions (*your advisor may be useful here*).
- Overview Charting the Course to show how the category fits into the Baldrige organizational framework and review other categories to show links.
- Review what category 7 results are the responsibility of your team.
- Review the scoring rubrics on pp. 54 and 55 of the criteria book.
- Pass out copies of your category from the Blazey self-assessment workbook from the book and CD *Insights to Performance Excellence in Education 2001* by Mark L. Blazey, Karen S. Davison, and John P. Evans, ASQ Quality Press and discuss how the workbook will be used at each meeting.
- Pass out copies of the data you collected related to your category.

- List each of the 11 Baldrige core values and concepts on a separate flip-chart sheet and brainstorm a bulleted list of specific things we do to support each core value (*refer to pp. 1-4 in the criteria book*).
- Begin going through each table or question for your category, writing out answers in the self-assessment workbook or identifying opportunities for improvement where there are no answers.
- Make recommendations about how opportunities for improvement could be met.
- Review agenda for the January meeting.
- End the meeting with a "plus-delta."

December:

- Send out minutes and/or updated material and plus-deltas from the November meeting.
- Plan for next meeting with your co-champion (*your advisor may be helpful here*).

January Team Meeting:

- Introductions and review the purpose of category teams.
- Check understanding of the minutes and/or updated material and any changes that have been made because of the November meeting plus-delta feedback.
- Pass out copies of the core values lists that were developed at the November meeting. Share lists from the other category teams and facilitate a review discussion.
- Pass out copies of any updated data to check for impact of improvements.
- Continue going through each table or question, writing out answers in your category self-assessment workbook, or identifying opportunities for improvement.

- Make recommendations about how opportunities for improvement could be met.
- Review agenda for the March meeting.
- End the meeting with a plus-delta.

February:

- Send out minutes and/or updated material and plus-deltas from the November meeting.
- Plan for next meeting with your co-champion (*your advisor may be helpful here*).

March Team Meeting:

- Introductions and review the purpose of category teams.
- Check understanding of the minutes and/or updated material and any changes that have been made because of the January meeting plus-delta feedback.
- Pass out copies of any updated data.
- Finish going through each table or question, writing out answers in your category self-assessment workbook, or identifying opportunities for improvement.
- Discuss how opportunities for improvement could be met.
- Complete your portion of Category 7: Organizational Performance Results.
- Have the team "score" your category and your portion of category 7 using the rubrics on pp. 54 and 55 of the criteria book.
- Thank members for their participation and discuss how the category team process could be improved next year.
- End the meeting with a plus-delta.

MEMO TO STAFF ON SHARED DECISION-MAKING AND CONDITIONS OF TEACHING

Memo

TO: Principals and Staff

FROM: Robert Ewy

RE: Clarifying the directions for the administration of the Shared Decision-Making, Conditions of Teaching, and District Shared Decision-Making

DATE: February 3, 2003

- FILL IN COLUMNS H AND I TO RECORD YOUR SCHOOL NUMBER
- FILL IN COLUMN J TO RECORD THE NUMBER OF YEARS IN THE DISTRICT
- USE PENCIL TO FILL IN ANSWERS
- MAY USE PEN FOR ESSAY QUESTIONS ONLY
- DO NOT STAPLE OR FOLD SURVEY

Both the Conditions of Teaching and the Shared Decision-Making surveys ask for anonymous feedback about recommendations for improvement. This feedback has proven very valuable at both the school and district level. For example, the Superintendent's Communication Council and the Classroom Teachers Council have worked together to analyze district recommendations and implement actions for improvement.

However, with anonymous feedback comes a responsibility to use that medium appropriately. Written recommendations for improvement should not single out or attack an individual, be sarcastic, be vengeful, or in any way be demeaning. One can certainly disagree with programs or practices and note that disagreement when writing recommendations for improvement. One can also relate frustrations and even anger about something that is not fair or just and do it in a way that does not violate the responsibility of anonymous feedback.

This issue was discussed with the CTC leadership and we agree that if the anonymous feedback responsibility is misused, the feedback will not be used when analyzing data. Please understand that the violation of the anonymous feedback responsibility has been very rare, but when it has happened, people have gotten unjustly and inappropriately hurt.

1. If you would rather not write on the back of the survey form, please use your computer to write your recommendations. Recommendations and the survey do not need to be connected to one another so please use whatever is most convenient for you to write your recommendations.

2. Secondly, please give your surveys and written recommendation(s) to your building CTC representative. He or she will turn them in to the district office for scoring. After scoring, all quantitative data and recommendations will then be returned to the building.

3. Survey forms will NOT be returned to the schools this year for transcribing the answers to essay questions. All comments from each school will be transcribed at the ESC and sent to that school as one report.

ALL SURVEYS SHOULD BE RETURNED NO LATER THAN **FEBRUARY 21.**

Thank you for the feedback you have provided in the past. We all look forward to your ideas for improvements in the future.

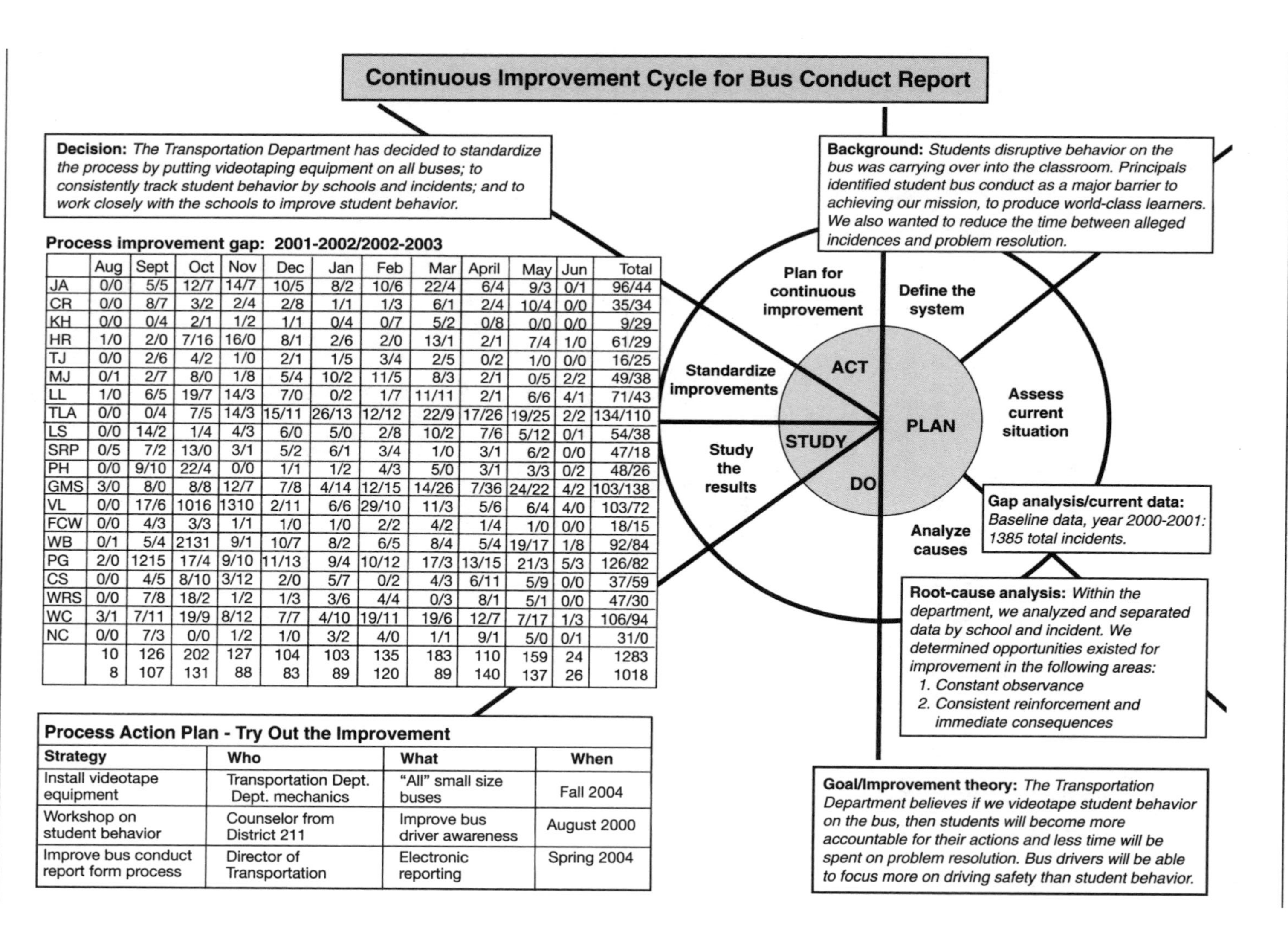

Process improvement gap: 2001-2002/2002-2003

	Aug	Sept	Oct	Nov	Dec	Jan	Feb	Mar	April	May	Jun	Total
JA	0/0	5/5	12/7	14/7	10/5	8/2	10/6	22/4	6/4	9/3	0/1	96/44
CR	0/0	8/7	3/2	2/4	2/8	1/1	1/3	6/1	2/4	10/4	0/0	35/34
KH	0/0	0/4	2/1	1/2	1/1	0/4	0/7	5/2	0/8	0/0	0/0	9/29
HR	1/0	2/0	7/16	16/0	8/1	2/6	2/0	13/1	2/1	7/4	1/0	61/29
TJ	0/0	2/6	4/2	1/0	2/1	1/5	3/4	2/5	0/2	1/0	0/0	16/25
MJ	0/1	2/7	8/0	1/8	5/4	10/2	11/5	8/3	2/1	0/5	2/2	49/38
LL	1/0	6/5	19/7	14/3	7/0	0/2	1/7	11/11	2/1	6/6	4/1	71/43
TLA	0/0	0/4	7/5	14/3	15/11	26/13	12/12	22/9	17/26	19/25	2/2	134/110
LS	0/0	14/2	1/4	4/3	6/0	5/0	2/8	10/2	7/6	5/12	0/1	54/38
SRP	0/5	7/2	13/0	3/1	5/2	6/1	3/4	1/0	3/1	6/2	0/0	47/18
PH	0/0	9/10	22/4	0/0	1/1	1/2	4/3	5/0	3/1	3/3	0/2	48/26
GMS	3/0	8/0	8/8	12/7	7/8	4/14	12/15	14/26	7/36	24/22	4/2	103/138
VL	0/0	17/6	1016	1310	2/11	6/6	29/10	11/3	5/6	6/4	4/0	103/72
FCW	0/0	4/3	3/3	1/1	1/0	1/0	2/2	4/2	1/4	1/0	0/0	18/15
WB	0/1	5/4	2131	9/1	10/7	8/2	6/5	8/4	5/4	19/17	1/8	92/84
PG	2/0	1215	17/4	9/10	11/13	9/4	10/12	17/3	13/15	21/3	5/3	126/82
CS	0/0	4/5	8/10	3/12	2/0	5/7	0/2	4/3	6/11	5/9	0/0	37/59
WRS	0/0	7/8	18/2	1/2	1/3	3/6	4/4	0/3	8/1	5/1	0/0	47/30
WC	3/1	7/11	19/9	8/12	7/7	4/10	19/11	19/6	12/7	7/17	1/3	106/94
NC	0/0	7/3	0/0	1/2	1/0	3/2	4/0	1/1	9/1	5/0	0/1	31/0
	10 8	126 107	202 131	127 88	104 83	103 89	135 120	183 89	110 140	159 137	24 26	1283 1018

Process Action Plan - Try Out the Improvement

Strategy	Who	What	When
Install videotape equipment	Transportation Dept. Dept. mechanics	"All" small size buses	Fall 2004
Workshop on student behavior	Counselor from District 211	Improve bus driver awareness	August 2000
Improve bus conduct report form process	Director of Transportation	Electronic reporting	Spring 2004

Figure A.1 PDSA example.

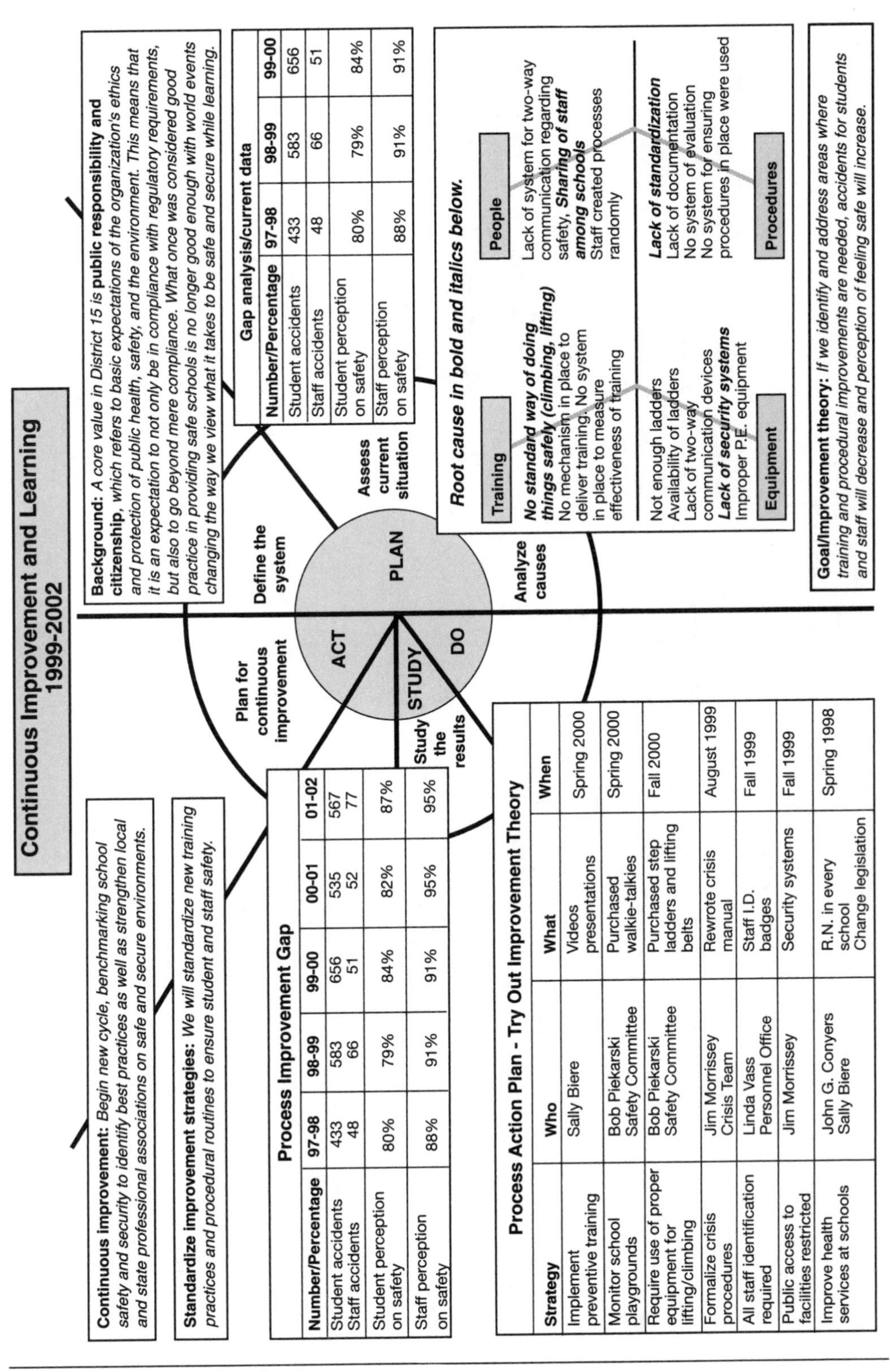

Process Improvement Gap

Number/Percentage	97-98	98-99	99-00	00-01	01-02
Student accidents Staff accidents	433 48	583 66	656 51	535 52	567 77
Student perception on safety	80%	79%	84%	82%	87%
Staff perception on safety	88%	91%	91%	95%	95%

Gap analysis/current data

Number/Percentage	97-98	98-99	99-00
Student accidents	433	583	656
Staff accidents	48	66	51
Student perception on safety	80%	79%	84%
Staff perception on safety	88%	91%	91%

Process Action Plan - Try Out Improvement Theory

Strategy	Who	What	When
Implement preventive training	Sally Biere	Videos presentations	Spring 2000
Monitor school playgrounds	Bob Piekarski Safety Committee	Purchased walkie-talkies	Spring 2000
Require use of proper equipment for lifting/climbing	Bob Piekarski Safety Committee	Purchased step ladders and lifting belts	Fall 2000
Formalize crisis procedures	Jim Morrissey Crisis Team	Rewrote crisis manual	August 1999
All staff identification required	Linda Vass Personnel Office	Staff I.D. badges	Fall 1999
Public access to facilities restricted	Jim Morrissey	Security systems	Fall 1999
Improve health services at schools	John G. Conyers Sally Biere	R.N. in every school Change legislation	Spring 1998

Figure A.2 PDSA example.

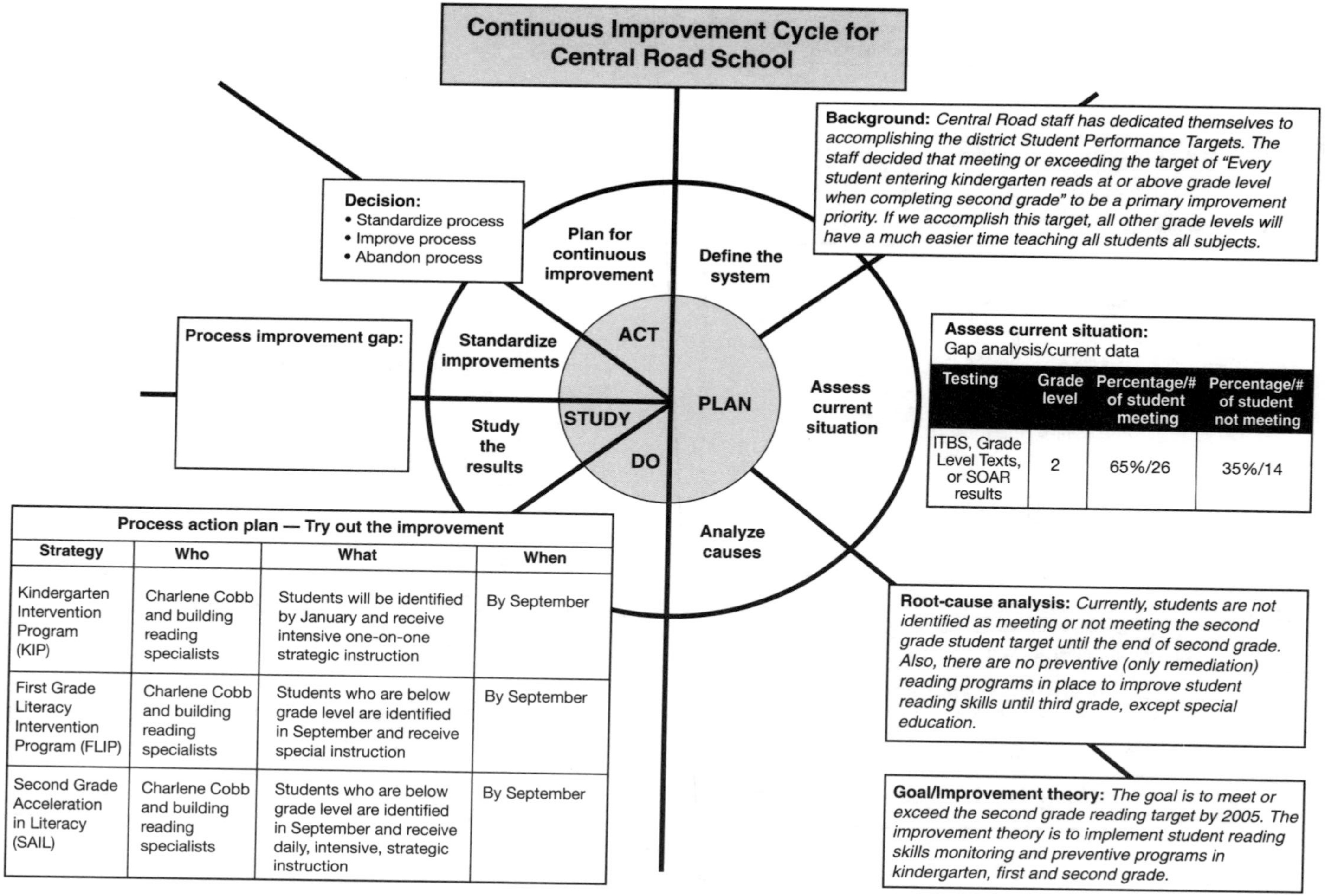

Continuous Improvement Cycle for Central Road School

Plan for continuous improvement
Define the system
Assess current situation
Analyze causes
Study the results
Standardize improvements
ACT
PLAN
DO
STUDY

Background: *Central Road staff has dedicated themselves to accomplishing the district Student Performance Targets. The staff decided that meeting or exceeding the target of "Every student entering kindergarten reads at or above grade level when completing second grade" to be a primary improvement priority. If we accomplish this target, all other grade levels will have a much easier time teaching all students all subjects.*

Assess current situation:
Gap analysis/current data

Testing	Grade level	Percentage/# of student meeting	Percentage/# of student not meeting
ITBS, Grade Level Texts, or SOAR results	2	65%/26	35%/14

Root-cause analysis: *Currently, students are not identified as meeting or not meeting the second grade student target until the end of second grade. Also, there are no preventive (only remediation) reading programs in place to improve student reading skills until third grade, except special education.*

Goal/Improvement theory: *The goal is to meet or exceed the second grade reading target by 2005. The improvement theory is to implement student reading skills monitoring and preventive programs in kindergarten, first and second grade.*

Decision:
- Standardize process
- Improve process
- Abandon process

Process improvement gap:

Process action plan — Try out the improvement

Strategy	Who	What	When
Kindergarten Intervention Program (KIP)	Charlene Cobb and building reading specialists	Students will be identified by January and receive intensive one-on-one strategic instruction	By September
First Grade Literacy Intervention Program (FLIP)	Charlene Cobb and building reading specialists	Students who are below grade level are identified in September and receive special instruction	By September
Second Grade Acceleration in Literacy (SAIL)	Charlene Cobb and building reading specialists	Students who are below grade level are identified in September and receive daily, intensive, strategic instruction	By September

Figure A.3 PDSA example.

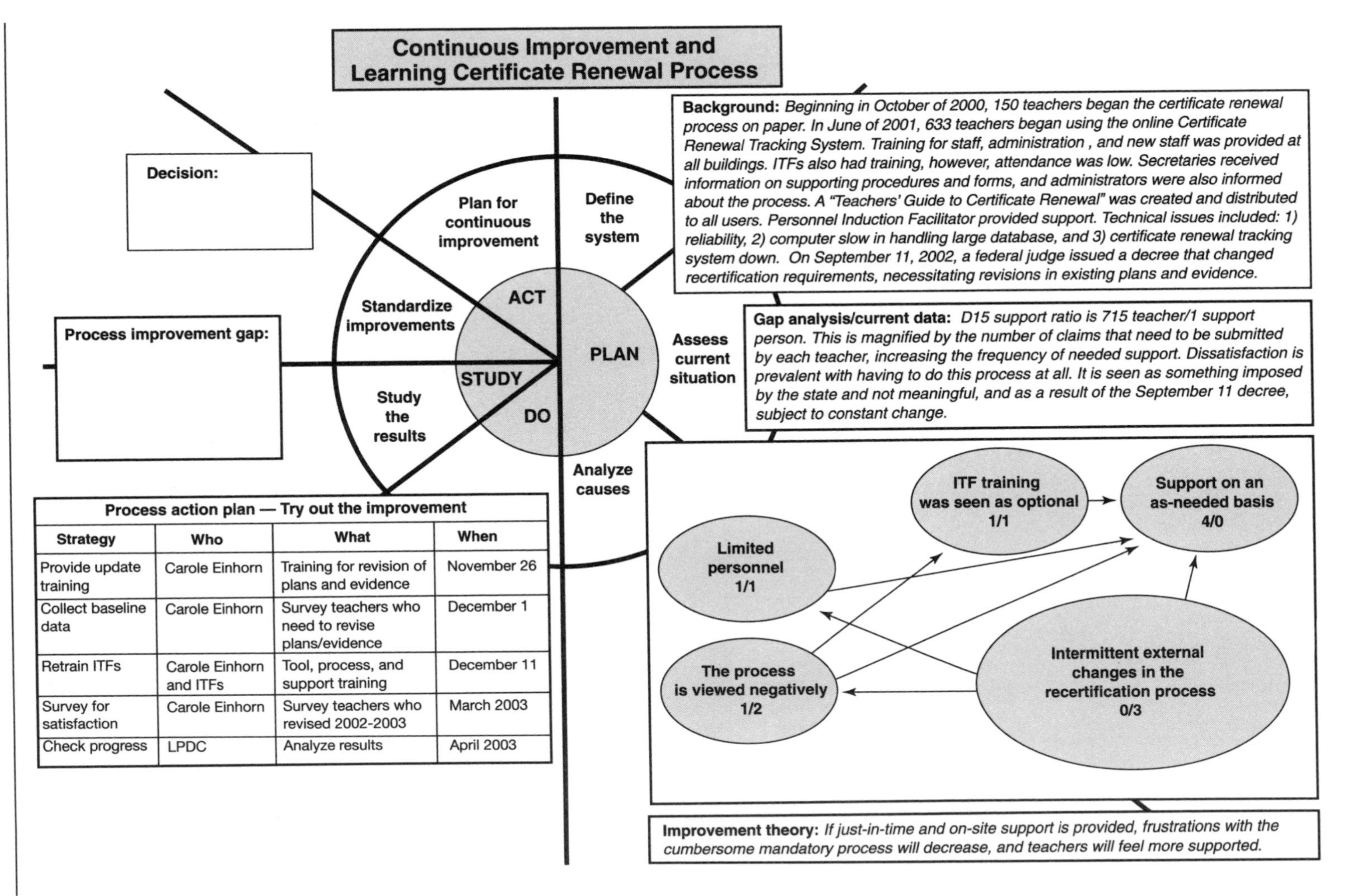

Figure A.4 PDSA example.

Appendix B

About District 15: An Overview

Community Consolidated School District 15 is a kindergarten through eighth-grade system of quality public education. The school district serves all or part of seven municipalities in northwest suburban Chicago. The district's 19 schools have been built or extensively remodeled over the past 14 years: 14 K-6, three junior high, one K-8, and one alternative school. Student enrollment for the 2002-2003 school year is 12,930, making District 15 the second largest elementary school district in Illinois.

The 2002-2003 budget is $146.9 million: 64.8 percent from local property taxes, 10.5 percent from state aid, 5.0 percent from state TRS, 2.9 percent from federal aid, 12.2 percent from transfers between funds, and 4.6 percent from other local sources. More than 90 percent of the operating budget is directly returned to the schools. The district operates its own transportation, custodial, maintenance, technology, and food service departments.

Our elementary classrooms are heterogeneously grouped with self-contained, team-taught, and multiage configurations. Our curriculum is standards-driven and aligned to state requirements. A balanced literacy framework guides instruction in reading and writing. Science is inquiry-based. Social science is experiential. Math emphasizes problem solving and authentic investigations. Specialists teach art, music, physical education, and fine arts in grades 1–8. Instrumental music instruction starts in grade 5.

At the junior-high level, writing is incorporated into every subject. Math includes pre-algebra and algebra. Life, biological, and physical sciences include hands-on labs in a technologically enriched environment. French, German, and Spanish foreign language instruction is offered.

District 15 provides programs for gifted and talented students from grades 3–8. Elementary students attend self-contained, multigrade classrooms where all subject areas are addressed. Some children may attend schools other than their assigned schools for this program. Gifted and talented seventh and eighth graders have differentiated curricula for language arts, social sciences, and mathematics.

Reading intervention programs are provided for students who are significantly below grade level in reading. These strategic, systematic, intensive programs—Kindergarten Intervention Program (KIP), First-grade Intervention Program (FLIP), and Second-grade Acceleration in Literacy (SAIL)—are designed to accelerate student achievement so that they will be reading at or above grade level by third grade. Soar to Success is a research-based program to help accelerate reading growth for children in grades 3-6 and Read 180, which combines sophisticated and motivating technology with high-interest, age-appropriate print materials, is used in junior-high schools and targeted elementary schools. One-on-one and small group interventions are provided for English Language Learners (ELL) students in grades K-8. Intervention programs for ELL students parallel the English language programs.

Child care before and after school is available in partnership with community park districts.

District 15 students participate in activities and competitions that include Junior Great Books, newspapers, First Lego League, Jason Project, Moonlink, Marslink, Journey North Tulip Project, yearbooks, Knowledge Masters, Science Olympiad, Young Authors' Conference, Chicago Tribune Spelling Bee, National Geography Contest, Odyssey of the Mind, Illinois Math League, Math Counts, science fairs, chess, drama, and sports.

Three junior-high and four elementary schools have earned the U.S. Department of Education Blue Ribbon Award for Excellence.

Among the district's 12,930 students are those with special needs that must be addressed, including some who do not speak English. A search of the data warehouse identifies 72 different languages spoken by the families of students who attend our schools. Approximately 25 percent of the district's students come from non-English speaking backgrounds, and many of those demonstrate limited English proficiency. Bilingual or ESL classes are offered to ELL students who qualify under Illinois State Board of Education (ISBE) guidelines.

Approximately 12.9 percent of our students are eligible for special education services. They include students with learning disabilities, behavioral and emotional disorders, physical or mental impairments, speech and language impairments, autism, and developmental delays. These students are served by full- and part-time special education teachers and related services staff such as school psychologists and social workers, occupational and physical therapists, adaptive physical education teachers, assistive technology specialists, hearing and vision teachers, a behavior specialist, and a music therapist.

District 15 also operates The Learning Academy, an alternative school that provides highly intensive programs for students from birth to 15 years of age who are eligible for special education or are at-risk for educational failure. The Learning Academy houses the only district-operated program in the state of Illinois that provides intervention services to children from birth to three years of age and a "second chance" program for students who consistently exhibit disruptive behaviors, receive repeated suspensions, or are in danger of expulsion.

Every school has a full-time nurse, a very unusual practice in Illinois and nationally. During the 2001-2002 school year, there were more than 94,627 student visits to health offices for accidents and illnesses and 56,854 student visits for medication administration. Student compliance for physical examinations and vaccinations was 99.1 percent, or almost two percent higher than the statewide compliance rate of 97.27 percent. In some cases, school nurses are the primary health care providers for our students.

Each year since 1996, junior high students with disabilities have participated in a week-long competition at the NASA Space Camp in Huntsville, Alabama, vying against nondisabled and gifted students from throughout the nation. Every year the students have finished first in at least one of four competition areas.

A high-performing staff, a key goal, is vital to the successful operation of the district and to producing world-class students. In the 2002-2003 school year, District 15 employed 1898 people: 947 are certified (teachers, social workers, psychologists, speech therapists, and other education professionals), 951 are classified staff, and 308 are certified substitutes. The teaching staff averages 15 years of experience. Sixty-five percent of certified staff members hold master's degrees. District 15 now has 40 national board-certified teachers, more than any other Illinois school district except Chicago. This year there are 18 candidates completing their applications/portfolios.

District 15's comprehensive four-year induction/mentoring program provides professional and personal support for newly hired teachers. This year, 92 experienced teachers served as mentor teachers in this nationally recognized program.

District 15 is at the forefront in the use of technology to enrich and enhance students' learning experiences. Computers in labs, wireless laptops on wheels, and classrooms and are used across the curriculum for data management information processing, word processing, presentations, spreadsheets, programming, design, research, and problem solving. Technology standards for grades K–8 drive instructional application in the classroom. Every regular classroom is equipped with a minimum of four computers, a 32" television monitor, a VCR, and a telephone on every teacher's desk. Students use computers extensively for writing projects, developing presentations, learning simulations, practicing skills, and research. Assistive technology services provide appropriate solutions to 63 students with special needs. District 15 students connect with the world around them through access to the Internet. Carefully structured Internet-based projects such as Moonlink and Marslink, an Internet space simulation, and the Jason Project, which studies ecology, geography, and different cultures, provide valuable information and interaction both with subject-matter experts and other students.

Video production studios in each school allow students to produce daily school news programs as well as other video projects. District 15's closed-circuit television network, Channel 44, broadcasts to all schools, enabling districtwide broadcasts of educational programming for staff development and special live productions such as Kids Vote/Election 2000, a real-world civics lesson centered on the Presidential election; live interviews with district visitors including legislators and former astronauts; and a District 15 teacher who exchanged science research data with students while participating in the Antarctica 2000 expedition.

The district is governed by a board of education consisting of seven members elected at large. The board's powers and duties include the broad authority to adopt and enforce all necessary policies for the management and governance of the public schools. Official action by board of education members must occur at a duly called and legally conducted meeting.

District 15 has dialogued with its stakeholder groups over time to determine what key requirements they want the district to deliver. These dialogues have verified the key requirements for each stakeholder group (see Table B.1).

Table B.1 Key requirements for stakeholders.

Stakeholder groups	Key requirements
Community members	To provide a world-class education, support the development of good community citizens, enhance property values, use property taxes efficiently, and maintain fiscal integrity.
Parents and PTA parents	To ensure a caring, safe, and orderly learning environment; provide well-qualified teachers in every classroom; provide a world-class education for every student; be informed about issues, events, programs, and practices in a timely manner; and learn in a respectful, cooperative environment.
Certified staff	To feel safe and secure in a caring work place, participate in decisions that directly affect their work, work in a healthy school climate, receive help and support when needed, be provided staff development that is relevant and of high quality, be informed in a timely manner, and receive recognition.
Support staff	To feel safe and secure in the work place, be treated with dignity and respect and feel supported by supervisors and peers, understand how job performance is measured and rewarded, be part of decision-making that relates to performance of duties, be provided staff development that is relevant and of high quality, work together as a team, and receive recognition.
Students	To learn in a caring, safe, and orderly environment, be treated by adults and peers respectfully and fairly, receive help when needed, behave according to expectations, do their best work, be satisfied with school, and be enthusiastic about what is learned and how it is learned.
Feeder high schools	To have students well prepared for high school and help determine high school preparation standards and expectations.
Businesses	To have employees who are well prepared for the workplace of the 21st century and have a voice in the standards and goals set for educating students.

District 15 has more than 3000 vendors that supply us with our needs.

The district has captured a 92 percent market share of the total number of students within its boundaries. Five schools located within the district boundaries are our main competition. Although competitors, these schools are also viewed as partners and are included in district activities as a means of connecting with the community to support all learners. District 15 understands there are reasons parents choose private and parochial schools, but the quality of education should not be one of them. Two requests to establish charter schools within the district's attendance boundaries have been received since charter school legislation was mandated in Illinois in 1996. In both cases, the groups withdrew upon reviewing the quality of education in the district and submitted their requests elsewhere. Parents of home-schooled children are not required to register with their public school so these data are not available.

Building on feedback gathered after District 15 became the first and only educational organization in the state of Illinois to earn the Lincoln Foundation Level III Award for Excellence in 1999, we continue to focus on continuous quality improvement as a method of aligning and integrating the management system. This approach calls for management by fact; implementation of the PDSA continuous improvement cycle at district, building, and classroom levels; and a results focus to ensure that all operations meet or exceed their defined targets.

In addition to serving as an effective management tool, the continuous quality improvement concept has also proved valuable as a teaching tool. Koalaty Kid, a student-centered approach to education that systematically applies the principles of total quality to the classroom, is now in place in all District 15 schools.

Producing world-class learners and building a connected learning community are construction projects that are never complete. This is why the district is committed to continuous quality improvement—so it will be prepared to provide the best possible education for the students of today as well as tomorrow. Based on extensive feedback and analysis, the following strategic challenges have been identified:

- **Population and diversity shifts:** The ethnic distribution of students in District 15 has shifted from approximately 80 percent white students in the 1992-

1993 school year to 66 percent in the 2002-2003 school year. Black, American Indian, and Asian populations have remained static, but our Hispanic student population has risen from 1279 to 2653 during the same 10-year span. Children from diverse backgrounds bring with them unique challenges to the education system, but our district celebrates the cultural diversity found within its boundaries. Because of our strong special education programs, parents are choosing District 15 as the district of choice to educate their child. Each of these challenges must be met by redesigning programs and practices and by reallocating resources.

- **Maintaining fiscal health and integrity:**
  Maintaining the quality of education in the face of continued revenue shortfalls is an increasingly critical challenge. School districts are neither inflation nor recession proof. Local property taxes are District 15's major source of revenue. Allocations from local property taxes represent 64.8 percent of the revenue. State funding provides approximately 10.5 percent. Our district has lost more than $15,900,000 over the past three years due to tax revenue refunds and credits. The state is reducing its contribution by approximately $2,000,000 in 2003 due to a huge state budget deficit.
- **Attracting and retaining a high-performing staff:**
  Assuring that a quality teaching staff is ready to teach our students is an increasingly difficult challenge each year. An average of 12 percent of the teaching staff and administration has been replaced each year over the past three years due to retirements and mobility. District 15 anticipates that the end of the 2003-2004 school year, it will have the largest number of retirees in district history. Nationally, the shortage makes competition for quality teachers and school leaders an issue the district has to continually address.
- **Striving for world-class learning:**
  District 15 has defined world-class learning to be the accomplishment of our student performance targets. The accomplishment of the student performance targets is something no other school district that we are aware of has achieved in total. Diversity shifts have

> given the "no significant differences" target special importance. With the board of education adopting this definition of world-class learning, District 15 has ambitious and clearly defined targets to assure that all students are prepared for a successful tomorrow.

By creating a Pareto diagram from community and staff feedback about district strategic challenges, we find that these four challenges represent 81 percent of the total number of responses received.

Additional descriptions of the district include:

- Approximately 13,000 volunteers donated more than 160,000 hours to District 15 schools during the 2002-2003 school year.
- District 15 operates its own bus fleet—one of the largest district-owned bus fleets in Illinois. Each day 143 buses safely transport 9715 parochial and public school children, logging 1.4 million miles each year.
- The Food Service Department served 1,038,825 meals during the 1999-2000 school year; 165,327 slices of pizza; and 1,016,555 cartons of milk. Food preparation center inspections are conducted by the local village two-to-four times per year. District 15 preparation centers averaged 97 out of the highest rating of 100. The village restaurant average is 87.
- Nearly 1.4 million square feet of floor space are cleaned and maintained every day. Twenty parking lots and play areas are plowed after every snowstorm. Approximately 76 acres of grass are mowed seasonally. Recycling efforts are under way at all facilities.

Results

- Annual resource center circulation for our schools tells us that District 15 students read an average of 49.25 books a year. Our community library circulation information shows that patrons read an average of 17. 39 books per year.
- Understanding to what degree students use logical-reasoning, problem-solving, and critical-thinking

skills is determined by analyzing the use of these thinking tools in the classroom. The greatest number of tools used (735) were to gather ideas, the second most often employed set of tools (399) were used to draw pictures of data, and the third most often-used tools (324) were used to connect ideas. Other tools expand thinking group ideas, sequence steps, track facts, and make decisions.

- Progress toward the goal of having 100 percent of District 15 students reading at or above grade level by the end of second grade has been steady. Currently 92 percent have achieved the goal.
- Out of 78 different grade-level testing areas and demographic group combinations, District 15 outperformed a comparative local school district in 60 out of 78 instances (77 percent), and outperformed the state in 75 out of 78 instances (96 percent).
- A sampling of District 15's student population in fourth and eighth grades participated in the first cycle of the World Class Tests. District 15 students outperformed an average of all other countries in mathematics and problem solving in both fourth and eighth grades.
- Student satisfaction with school has improved in five of the six past years. ELL student satisfaction with school is 10 percent higher than the all-student average.
- By tracking students who attended District 15 schools from second to sixth grade using the Iowa Test of Basic Skills NCE scores, we find they achieve our 90 percent achievement target.
- District 15 tracks student enthusiasm for learning by grade level and subject area. Enthusiasm for learning has moved from the 30 percent range in fifth and eighth grade to the 80 percent range.
- 87 percent of District 15 parents give schools a grade of A or B, 92 percent of our special education parents give schools the same grades, and 84 percent of our bilingual parents give an A or B grade to the schools.

- For every percentage point of performance on the state test, it costs District 15 $111.93 versus the state's average expenditure of $130.70 per percentage point of performance.
- 48 District 15 teachers have received National Board for Professional Teaching Standards (NBPTS) certification (40 of these are currently on staff). Chicago is the only school district in Illinois with more nationally board certified teachers.
- Certified and support staff satisfaction has improved over the past five years to about 90 percent.
- 13 major support processes have significantly reduced their cycle times over the past two years using the PDSA cycle.
- Daily bus on-time delivery is at or above 98 percent.
- The transportation department has been recognized as one of 50 Great Fleets Across America by *School Bus Fleet* magazine.
- Satisfaction with custodial services is at 4.5 on a 5 point scale or a 90 percent satisfaction level.
- Volunteers logged more than 160,000 thousand hours of service. Calculating the number of volunteer hours at the average hourly rate of pay for program assistants shows that volunteers represent a $1.66 million dollar contribution of services to District 15.
- 88 percent of community residents would recommend to friends that they move into our district so their children could attend our schools.
- A recent survey indicates prospective teachers are attracted to District 15 because of our quality reputation, supportive environment, salary and benefits, and our outstanding mentoring program.
- No grievances have gone to arbitration since 1986; only two have gone beyond step one.
- District 15 was the first district in the nation to receive the National School Boards Association/ Institute for the Transfer of Technology to Education Reed Hundt Award for Excellence in Technology.

Nautical References

Beavis, Bill, and Richard G. McCloskey. 1995. *Salty dog talk: The nautical origins of everyday expressions.* Dobbs Ferry, N.Y.: Sheridan House.

Bits & pieces. Chicago: Lawrence Ragan Communications, Inc.

Chapman, Charles F. 1975. *Piloting, seamanship, and small boat handling,* 51st edition. New York: The Hearst Corporation.

Encyclopedia of nautical knowledge. 1994. Centreville, MD: Cornell Maritime Press.

Eyges, Leonard. 1989. *The perfect pilot: Coastal navigation by eye, intuition, and common sense.* Camden, MA: International Marine Publishing Company.

Hendrickson, Robert. 1994. *Salty words.* New York: William Morrow and Company.

Herreshoff, Halsey C. 1983. *The sailor's handbook.* London: Marshall Editions Ltd.

Isil, Olivia A. 1996. *When a loose cannon flogs a dead horse there's the devil to pay.* Camden, Maine: International Marine/Ragged Mountain Press.

Jeans, Peter D. 1998. *An ocean of words: A dictionary of nautical words and phrases.* Secaucus, N.J.: Carol Publishing Group.

Rousmaniere, John. 1989. *The Annapolis book of seamanship*, 2nd edition. New York: Simon and Schuster.

Index

C

M

N

O